Rosanna of the Amish tells the unusual story of an Irish Catholic baby, Rosanna McGonegal, who was reared by Elizabeth Yoder, an unmarried Amish lady.

The author, Rosanna's son, reveals how she was initiated into Amish ways and adopted their strange customs and practices.

You will enjoy reading about—

- Rosanna's deep affection for Momly.
- Her first husking bee and singing.
- Little Crist's nighttime visits to Rosanna.
- Detailed descriptions of German preaching services and how the Amish choose their ministers.
- The inside story of Amish weddings and funerals.
- Rosanna's belief in powwowing.
- The importance of simple dress, hard work, and good food.

This book portrays simply and honestly the religious, social, and economic traditions the Amish have followed for more than 275 years.

ROSANNA
OF THE AMISH

JOSEPH W. YODER

Illustrated by George Daubenspeck

HERALD PRESS
Scottdale, Pennsylvania
Waterloo, Ontario

The paper used in this publication is recycled and
meets the minimum requirements of American
National Standard for Information Sciences—
Permanence of Paper for Printed Library Materials,
ANSI Z39.48-1984.

ROSANNA OF THE AMISH
Revised edition, copyright © 1973 by Herald Press,
Scottdale, Pa. 15683; published simultaneously in
Canada by Herald Press, Waterloo, Ont. N2L 6H7
International Standard Book Number: 0-8361-1714-X
Printed in the United States of America

Thirty-eighth printing, 1996
382,500 copies in print of all editions

Dedicated
to
My Mother
Rosanna McGonegal Yoder

Contents

List of Illustrations

Preface

The author begs to explain that he was inspired to write this present volume, ROSANNA OF THE AMISH, by the fact that several writers with vivid imaginations and little regard for facts have written books about the Amish and have missed almost entirely the cardinal virtues of this people. Some of them have exaggerated a certain characteristic out of all proportion and have made even a virtue look ridiculous. Their object seemed to be to write an unusual story rather than to adhere to the truth.

Having been born of Amish parents and having grown to manhood as an Amish boy, the author knows the Amish people intimately. In fact, he is one of them, and knows their customs and practices socially, economically, and religiously, in minute detail.

All the episodes in ROSANNA OF THE AMISH are based on fact. Every name in the book is the real name of the person mentioned, and the story is the actual life story of Rosanna. Instead of holding the Amish, a very devout people, up to ridicule as some writers apparently delight to do, the author desires to tell the truth about them, setting forth their virtues, and they have many, as well as their peculiarities. The fact is that what seems like a peculiarity to the outsider becomes a virtue when one's experience enables him to understand the underlying motives and principles.

The author knew personally every principal character in the book except Simeon Riehl whose name is fictitious. The O'Connor boys and Rosanna's parents were the author's ancestors, and he has tried according to his early training to portray them just as he knew them, truthfully. Every ceremony and service is described exactly as it takes place and as it is carried out and has been carried out practically unchanged for more than two hundred and seventy-five years.

CHAPTER 1

The Voyage

THE potato fields of Ireland were already waving their luxurious growth of green on that hot afternoon in June early in the nineteenth century as big John O'Connor leaned on his spade in deep meditation. He had been to the village tavern the evening before and had heard Tim O'Tool tell of the wonderful opportunities in America. Tim had just returned from a three-year sojourn in the new country and with many a gesture of head and hand he told of the easy jobs to be had in America.

"Why, could you believe it biys," said Tim, "all I iver did was carry bricks up three stories, and a man up there, sure he did all the work?"

It was the freedom and the opportunities that John O'Connor was thinking about. He had been to the village just yesterday to see Sandy McGinnis about learning the blacksmith trade and was told, "You're a farmer's son, ain't ye? Then why do you come here wantin' to be a blacksmith? Home wid ye and do your faither's bidding—a farmer is what the likes o' you is calculated to be."

Those words, "A farmer is what the likes o' you is calculated to be," were ringing in his ears and burning in his heart ever since. I guess it's true if I stay in these parts, he mused, but America! What did Tim O'Tool say about America? Why sez 'e, "In America a man can be whativer he has a mind to." Why should I wear out my young life settin' potatoes in Ireland when I might be ownin' a business in America? As he resumed his work, speeding up a bit to make up for his meditations, he overtook his younger brother William and called out to him, "Step aside, me biy, you're interferin' with the progress of a prosperous American businessman."

"American businessman, me eye," said William in wide-eyed wonder.

"Well, may the saints be blessin' ye. Might you be having a job for your humble servant and kinsman, also of Irish descent, Mr. Prosperous Business American Man, or whativer it is ye aire?"

That evening at the supper table, when the meal was well under way, John O'Connor addressed his father thoughtfully and said, "Faither, is it not the rule of Ireland that a son must engage in the same business as his faither? Sandy McGinnis told me as much yisterday when I asked him if he would be good enough to teach me to be a blacksmith. 'A farmer is what the likes o' you is calculated to be,' he snarled as though I was a blockhead and he was teachin' me The Rule o' Three. But at the tavern last night Tim O'Tool, who has just returned from America, said that there are no family rules nor trade rules over there, and a young man may choose any work he fancies. Faither, I've been thinkin' all day that if you and mither are willing, I'll be sailin' for America the last o' the month. Tim says the harvest will be on then and they'll be needin' a lot of cradlers. By workin' in the harvestfield I could earn enough to tide me over while I looked for a trade that suited me fancy." As John spoke, his mother rose from the table and busied herself about the stove to hide the tears that were beginning to trickle down her cheeks.

The father heard in silence all John said, and it was not surprising to him. John was an excellent worker, always taking the heaviest tasks cheerfully. But he knew that John did his work as a dutiful son, that he never wanted to be a farmer, and that his heart was in learning a trade or in business. These words kindled the fires of love and admiration in the father's eyes as he looked at his broad shouldered son, so much like himself and said, "Me biy, it would be no light matter for me and your mither to see you breakin' the family circle like that, but what you say is the truth and we would not be standin' in your way. You're a likely lad and in great free America you'll have a chance to rise to the top and some day your mither and me will be proud of our son, a prosperous American businessman. May the saints bless you."

As the father spoke these words of seeming finality, Bridget, the only daughter in the family and next to John in age, could no longer conceal her emotions. She wept audibly as she hid her face in her apron.

"Don't be screechin' the likes o' that, Bridget, for someday you'll be comin' to America to see me," John said, and there was more truth in those words than he then suspected.

John had scarcely finished speaking when William, just three years younger than John and possessing a fine sense of Irish wit and humor, spoke. "Faither, don't you think that the Elder Brother will be needin' a bodyguard among those fierce American Indians, and don't you think it advisable for me to join the colonies with him?"

The father looked at William with a slight twinkle in his eye, trying to keep back a tear rising in sympathy with Bridget and her mother. He said, "A bodyguard for John would no be a bad idea. If John is willing to have ye clutterin' after him, I suppose we might as well let you go now as later. It will be hard for you to conform to the customs of Ireland and be a farmer when there are so many opportunities in America for work and so much liberty in choosing what pleases you."

"You see," said William, "I have much experience as a bodyguard, for have I not driven that varmit of a Pat

McGonegal off the place when he came here a-courtin'
Bridget? Come on, Bridget, and stop your blubberin'
and tell your faither that you're willing to give me a recommendation as a first-class bodyguard."

At the thought of giving William a recommendation
as a bodyguard, Bridget could not help smiling through
her tears. "You may be pokin' fun at me, William, but
it's no small affair to have your big brother crossin' that
awful ocean. As for Pat McGonegal, I think I can take
care of him myself without any bodyguard from you."

"Aye, Bridget," said John, "there's entirely too much
truth in what you say. If you iver marry that Pat Mc-
Gonegal you'll be having to take care o' him, for I don't
believe that lazy spalpeen will iver be able to take care
o' you."

When the family circle had agreed that John and William should sail for America, the news of their going
spread rapidly. As they worked hard in the field to help
father all they could before leaving, passers-by frequently hailed them with "Safe journey and good luck
in America." The older men would always add, "And
may the saints bless you."

Time passed almost too rapidly, for there was much
washing and mending and many preparations to make
for the great journey. Finally, the last day of June arrived, and bidding their parents good-by, they made
their way to the harbor where the great steamship, *Nor-
mandy,* lay at anchor. They soon booked passage for
New York and were off to America, the land of opportunity.

Tim O'Tool had told them about the great coal mining interests at Scranton, and on the weary voyage they
had plenty of time to decide that Scranton in Pennsylvania should be their destination. On the boat they met
other young men from Ireland and England and Scotland who were out to seek their fortunes. Luckily for

John and William they met up with James MacDonald from Scotland, who was on his way to Scranton. He had been there before and offered to pilot the boys to their destination.

Scranton was in the heart of Pennsylvania's hard coal fields and the boys had no trouble finding work. There were houses to build, streets to grade, water systems to lay, and coal to mine, to say nothing of job opportunities in stores and factories and hotels.

John O'Connor was a big man. He was six feet two inches tall and weighed two hundred and ten pounds, all muscle and sinew. In the White Horse Hotel one night he helped the landlord throw out three husky and unruly sons of Hungary, whereupon the landlord hired John to tend the bar. The wages were good and in comparison to Ireland, John felt that he was rapidly becoming a prosperous American businessman.

William O'Connor, slighter than John somewhat and wittier, with the sunshine of Killarney always embellishing his smile, happened at mass one Sunday morning to fall into conversation with Patrick O'Harra, who operated a large store in Scranton. Mr. O'Harra was so delighted with the ready wit and Irish brogue of William that he was moved to say, "And what are you doin' here, me biy?"

William replied that he was looking for work but that he was not much interested in mining coal.

"Well," said Mr. O'Harra, "I have a general store down on Main Street. Come down in the mornin' and look the place over and if you like the setup, I might be findin' something for you to do. It's the Irish, you know, that have the will to work and advance."

William showed some interest in the idea but not too much. He didn't want to give the idea that he was very anxious for a job in a good store. But he lost no time in seeing John at the hotel and telling him with uncontrollable joy that he too was on the rapid road to becoming a "prosperous American businessman."

William appeared at the store the next morning early enough to have the appearance of punctuality and late enough not to appear too anxious for the job. He greeted the proprietor with, "The top o' the mornin' to ye, Mr. O'Harra, and it's a fine place you're havin' here."

The lilt of his Irish brogue and the sunshine of Killarney in his smile caught Mr. O'Harra's admiration and confidence. The hiring of William O'Connor as a clerk in his large store was only a matter of pleasant conversation. William worked hard and was conscientious about the smallest details, so it was no wonder that he was promoted rapidly until he was head clerk. He was even sent to New York by himself to buy goods for the growing store. How he welcomed these opportunities of broadening his knowledge of merchandising, for he had resolved deep in his heart that he would not always be a clerk. Much as he liked Mr. O'Harra, someday he would have a store of his own, and then, what a glorious thought, "Maybe faither and mither and Bridget would be comin' over to join the prosperous sons in America."

John and William had already talked this joyous prospect over, for, while William was going forward in merchandising, John was making strides in the hotel business. Not satisfied to tend the bar and be the master bouncer when some poor addict became uncontrollable, John decided to lease a hotel he had heard about and go into business for himself. But he needed a woman to take general charge of the house. Why couldn't Bridget come over and do that for him?

It was three years now since he and William had left home, and Bridget was now a full-grown woman. Had not mother written from time to time that Pat McGonegal was more insistent upon marrying her than ever? Here would be a good chance to get her away from him; so he wrote to Bridget, enclosed a check for more than her fare, and begged her to come. He did not mention this strategy against Pat McGonegal to Bridget, but he wrote to his mother secretly and urged the plan. He explained that in America there were many up and coming young men who would admire Bridget's beauty and Irish charm and who would make fine husbands for her.

When the letter arrived with the check urging Bridget to come to America, painting in glowing colors the possibilities of a fine home and a prosperous husband, the family agreed that America was her great opportunity too. In due time Bridget O'Connor with a few other girls from Killarney came to America to seek their homes, their husbands, and their fortunes.

To make the journey a little easier, John met Bridget in New York as the great steamship docked in the harbor. John recognized Bridget as he met her and her companions, and reaching out his hand in welcome said, "Hello, Bridget, my dear. How beautiful you have grown. Why the rose of Killarney is on your cheeks, the music of her birds in your voice, and the blue of her skies is in your eyes. Bridget O'Connor, if ye weren't me own sister, I'd be fallin' in love wid ye meself."

"Go along wid ye, John O'Connor. It's just Irish blarney you're givin' me, and I don't believe a word of it."

John was introduced to Bridget's companions, and they all boarded a train for Scranton, a jolly Irish group. On the way John managed to find out from Bridget everything about father and mother and whether they would consider coming to America.

That evening William, dressed in the latest style, came over to Hotel Killdare to see his sister and find out all he could about father and mother and his good

friends in Ireland. The joy of luring Bridget far away
from Pat McGonegal, having her with them, the presence of the other Irish girls, their brogue and wit and
humor, all made the evening a joy to the rising O'Connor boys.

CHAPTER 2

The Birth of Rosanna

BRIDGET, who had always helped her mother at
home, sharing the responsibility, found no trouble in
managing the household duties of her brother John's
Hotel Killdare. This hostelry soon built up a reputation
for good food, clean beds, and an orderly barroom.
John O'Connor's business began to thrive far beyond
his fondest dreams. Bridget was doing the work well.
But imagine John's surprise and consternation while
walking down the street one day to see Pat McGonegal
coming toward him.

"Why, hello, Pat," said John, greatly surprised.
"What brings you to America?"

"Well, it's a foin question you're askin' me, and a
foin answer it is that I have for ye. I've come to America to marry Bridget O'Connor. You may know the lady;
I believe she's related to you by rather close family ties.
You broad-shouldered son of St. Patrick. You thought
you'd separate us by that little stream called the Atlantic Ocean, but it might do you good to know that I was
thinkin' of comin' to America on me own accord. And
when Bridget came, all the king's horses and all the
king's men could not a-kept me from comin.' You
know, John O'Connor, that I have always been deeply
in love with Bridget. She's the only girl in the world I'd

be livin' for, and by the holy cross of St. Michaels, I'll die for her if called upon to do it."

John stood amazed as he heard these unequivocal words of Patrick McGonegal, whom he had not seen for three years or more and who by now had grown into rugged manhood. Pat was not as tall as John O'Connor, but he was built from the ground up. John sized him up and decided he would not force Pat to fight for her, not if John was to be the other contestant. John could hardly believe what he saw and heard in Pat—a man of resolution, determination, self-control, and confidence.

At last John found his voice and said, "Pat, you'll be rememberin' that in the auld country I was against ye, but as I see you and hear you now here in free America with all its opportunities, I've changed me mind; I believe that since you have shown gumption enough to cross the ocean for Bridget, you will have gumption enough to be a good husband for her. That is all I am interested in."

"Sure, it's a good husband I'll be to her. Who could be less for a girl like Bridget—the beauty of Killarney written all over her face, and the blessed St. Cecilia herself putting music into her voice. John, she's the only perfect woman I've iver seen."

John extended his powerful right hand and taking Pat by the hand said, "You and Bridget it shall be, Pat. You have my consent and my blessing. I'm running Hotel Killdare on the next block; you'll find Bridget there and you are welcome at any time."

"John O'Connor, it's a great favor and blessing that you're conferrin' on me this day. By all the Saints in Ireland, I swear you shall never regret what you have just said."

Pat hurried off to Hotel Killdare where Bridget was supervising the evening meal. He stepped into the parlor and asked a waitress to call Bridget. When Bridget

came and saw Pat, better dressed than she had ever
seen him before, she flushed with surprise and delight.

"Why, Pat McGonegal, where in the world did you
come from and how did you ever get here?"

Pat reached out his hand and taking hers said, "Bridget O'Connor, I've just come from me native country,
beautiful Ireland. I waded the Atlantic Ocean by the aid
of a steamship. I shipped from New York on the fastest
train I iver saw, and I came to Scranton, Hotel Killdare,
to see the most beautiful girl in the world, Mistress
Bridget O'Connor by name. Is me explanation clear?"
The love light in Bridget's eyes assured Pat that he was
treading on safe ground, and together with John's consent and blessing he was filled with an inward happiness
that almost ruined his studied control.

During the last few years Pat had worked in the iron
ore mines of Cornwall, England; so it was not surprising
when he heard of the iron ore mines in Centre County,
Pennsylvania, in the Half Moon Valley not far from
Bellefonte, that he at once headed for the mines. He
was reluctant to leave Bridget after seeing her for only a
few minutes, but he wanted to prove to John O'Connor
that he, too, came to America to take advantage of the
many opportunities for work. He would not let himself
look like a slacker now. When Pat arrived in Bellefonte,
he went first to see the priest, Father O'Day, to get instruction in American ways of living and directions on
how to get to the ore mines. When he arrived in Half
Moon Valley, he had no trouble obtaining work, but he
did have some difficulty finding room and board. The
settlement was rather small and the Irish Catholic families had their rooms all filled. The Irish foreman came
to his rescue.

Said Sandy McGuire, "Me biy, there's no room
among our own folk, but there's another class of people
livin' hereabouts that are mighty foin. They are the

Amish farmers. They're a bit peculiar lookin'. The men wear long hair, big beards, broad-brimmed hats, and the women wear black kerchiefs around their heads, and long capes instid o' coats, but they set a good table and they put their religion into their everyday lives. You'll not be needin' to hide valuables in their homes."

Pat started out to find a boarding place among the Amish. The first Amishman he met was Reuben Kauffman, a sturdy young man with slight chin beard and long hair. Pat was amused at the peculiar costume, but he concealed his curiosity and said, "Neighbor, I'm a stranger in this country and I'm looking for a boarding place, could you tell me of one?"

"Yes, sir," said Reuben. "Miss Elizabeth Yoder, who lives near the mines, sometimes takes boarders."

Pat soon found the place. Elizabeth Yoder was an unmarried lady, large of stature, and very capable. When Pat asked her whether she could accommodate him with board and room, she paused a moment and then said in a low, well-modulated voice, "I sometimes take a roomer, and if you think it will be good enough for you, I think I could give you board and room."

Pat found the work in this mine easier than in the Cornwall mine and the pay considerably better. His happiness grew as he learned more about American ways of living. He soon saw, too, that with the low rents in Half Moon Valley, and the reasonable cost of food bought from Amish farmers, it would not be long till he could marry Bridget, rent a house, and have a home of his own. He soon learned to confide in Elizabeth Yoder, and it was a pleasure to tell her about Bridget and his plans. Her counsel always seemed so sound and sensible.

After working at the mines a little less than a year, he said to Elizabeth one evening, "Elizabeth, I'm thinkin' a bit of marrying in June and bringing Bridget here. There is nothing in the world I want so much as to have Bridget near me. Work is good, and the Half Moon Valley is almost as beautiful as Killarney. What do you think?"

"Other men no better off than you get married," she replied. "Why can't you? Where there's a will there's a way."

To Pat that was approval. Knowing that houses were scarce Elizabeth said, "If you want to get married in June, you can bring your wife here a while till you can find a house." That was the very inducement Pat wanted, and that settled it.

Pat and Bridget now exchanged many letters getting ready for the wedding in June. They would be married in the church, and John, who was very fond of his sister, would invite a score of friends to his hotel dining room for the wedding dinner. The dining room would be decorated with orange blossoms and June roses, and it would be a real wedding. A few days before the wedding was to take place, Pat came to Scranton. He bought himself a fine black suit for the wedding and Bridget a beautiful dress of white silk and a long white veil.

On the chosen day they gathered at the church, the priest said the solemn rites and pronounced them husband and wife. The dinner party was resplendent with choice foods, a beautiful bouquet of flowers, a drap o' wine and much gayety. The brothers, John and William, tried to be gay with all their friends, but they could not quite conceal a bit of sadness in having their beautiful sister taken away from them.

The newlyweds took the afternoon train for Philadelphia to visit some friends. After a few happy days they returned to Bellefonte and their new home in Half

Moon Valley. For a few months they lived with Elizabeth Yoder, accepting her offer that Pat bring his new wife to her home until he found a house in which to live.

These two women, so differerent, became fast friends. Bridget was a buxom Irish girl with quick wit and fluent speech; Elizabeth was tall and rugged, plain of dress and slow of speech. She always wore a white cap tied beneath her chin, a kerchief folded tightly about her waist and breast, a plain dress, and an apron. She generally spoke in short sentences but when she spoke she always seemed to say something that stimulated Bridget's courage or deepened her confidence. Bridget was happy in this quaint, unadorned home where simplicity and sincerity were natural forms of religion.

Often these two women sat of an afternoon planning Bridget's new home. Elizabeth would tell how to plant and care for a garden, how to can fruits and vegetables, how to dry corn and tomatoes for the winter, how to raise chickens and have her own eggs, how to make tallow candles and soap, and many other things that would save an outlay of money. With the Amish, thrift is not religion, but it is a next door neighbor, so Elizabeth was able and glad to give Bridget many ideas that would make her housekeeping less expensive, and would enable them to save some of Pat's earnings every month. One of the Amish mottoes is, "Spend less than you earn and you'll never be in debt."

After several months of boarding, a house was vacated and Pat immediately put in his application for it. It was late in October when the trees on the mountain sides were turning from green to gold and brown that the McGonegals with the aid of Elizabeth moved into their little home. It was not far away; so these two women whose friendship grew with the passing days visited back and forth frequently.

Pat, too, was not forgetful of Elizabeth's kindness to him. Many times when the wintry snows were filling the air he could be seen at her woodpile sawing and splitting firewood and carrying it in for her. Sometimes Elizabeth walked over to Bridget with a basket on her arm filled with doughnuts and half-moon (dried apple) pies and maybe a jar of tomatoes or a head of cabbage. The two women seemed to complement each other—Bridget's Irish sunshine shed a ray of joy into Elizabeth's somber life, while Elizabeth's calm reserve gave Bridget poise and assurance.

Time sped rapidly in the Half Moon Valley. By day the song of industry cheered the inhabitants and by night the whippoorwill and the katydid filled the air with bedtime melodies. The years passed rapidly and Pat and Bridget became the parents of a growing family. How Elizabeth rejoiced at each new arrival. First came Margaret, a year later William, and two years after that John. So deep was Bridget's love and respect for her two fine brothers that she named her sons after them. Two years after John was born came another girl, Rosanna. How glad Bridget was for this second baby girl, but alas, she was not privileged to enjoy Rosanna for long. Complications set in. Elizabeth cared for Bridget during her illness, but five days after the birth of Rosanna, Bridget died.

It was a terrible blow to Pat to be left with four little motherless children, and one only five days old. Again Elizabeth came to his rescue. With the aid of a few of the Catholic women, Elizabeth made all the preparations for the funeral. Elizabeth at once took the little baby, Rosanna, over to her own house where she could care for her and let her rest where it was quiet.

After the funeral, Pat came to see the baby and plan with Elizabeth what seemed best to do. After considering first one plan and then another, Pat said, "Elizabeth, I believe I can take the three older children to Philadelphia where my friends will give them homes, but how in the world can I take a nine-day-old baby so far?"

"You are right, Pat. Rosanna is too young to take so far. If you want me to, I'll keep her for you till you find a place for the other children. Then when she is a little older you can come and get her."

"The Saints be praised," said Pat. "Nothing in the world would suit me better."

As soon as Pat could, he disposed of his household goods. Reuben Kauffman offered to take Pat and the three children to Bellefonte where they could catch a train to Philadelphia. Just a little over seven years ago, Pat remembered, he had hired a livery-man to bring him and his new bride to Half Moon Valley, and what unspeakable joy had filled their hearts. But today he was leaving the broad peaceful valley and his heart was very heavy.

As the horses trotted along light-footed and spirited, they neared the entrance to the valley where the road leads between the mountains. Pat knew that when he passed the next turn in the road the valley would be lost from his view, maybe forever. As they neared the turn Pat looked back once more to the little cemetery on the hillside, which now held the most priceless possession he had ever known. In spite of the presence of Reuben and the children, tears rolled down his cheeks.

With a voice as steady as possible, he turned to Reuben and said, "You'll be excusin' me, Reuben, but me heart is terribly pained to leave her there on the hillside alone, who was so young and beautiful. I'm glad Elizabeth is keepin' Rosanna. If iver there was a woman who had the qualities of the blessed Virgin Mary, it is Elizabeth Yoder. Reuben, ye'll be takin' a little interest in Rosanna too, won't you?"

By now they had passed Beaver's Gap and were rapidly approaching Bellefonte, nestled among the foothills of the Alleghenies. When they had taken the children and a few little bundles from the spring wagon, Pat turned to Reuben and asked, "Now, what do I owe you, Reuben, for bringing us out?"

"Nothing at all," said Reuben. "We Amish folks are always glad to help our neighbors when they are in need, but not for money."

Pat insisted on paying, but Reuben was adamant. "Well, Reuben, if you won't take any pay, accept my everlasting gratitude and believe me, I'll always be praying that the Holy Virgin will be blessin' ye with peace and prosperity."

Reuben did not know much about the blessings of the Holy Virgin, but from the way Pat said it, and from the gratitude in Pat's eyes, Reuben knew Pat wished him well. These two men, so different, had become fast friends—the one a plain Amishman faithful to the rules of his church, simplicity of attire, unworldliness; the other, a Roman Catholic, faithful to his church, the Rosary and the Confessional. What a compliment to both these groups differing so widely in religion, that they lived in perfect peace and mutual respect in the fair Half Moon Valley. The Amish farmers supplied the Catholic miners with food; the Catholic iron ore miners provided the Amish farmers with a market for what they produced. Each complemented the other. Different? Yes, but much alike in one thing, faithfulness to his own church.

Reuben stood on the station platform watching the train bearing Pat and his three children away. As the train glided down along the winding stream and out into the great Penn's Valley it was finally lost to view. Reuben, turning to untie his horses for the journey home, said half aloud and half to himself, "Sorry to see Pat McGonegal go away. He's a good man."

CHAPTER 3

The Lost Creek Valley

TO earn a little spending money, Elizabeth Yoder frequently cooked for Amish threshing crews. Sometimes when farmers were short of men in the harvest field, she would even help to bind sheaves. It was well known that it took a good man to bind more wheat or oats in a day than Elizabeth could. It generally took two men to "take up" after a cradle, but on a few occasions she volunteered to do it herself, and to the amazement of the men, she did not lose a single sheaf.

It was not unusual among the Amish farmers to have the women who could be spared from household chores do the lighter work in the hayfield, the harvest field and cornhusking. But when it came to unpleasant farm work like spreading lime, loading manure, or threshing, the women were never asked to help. One of the crowning virtues among the Amish, however, is to be able to do hard work rapidly and skillfully and without complaint. A slow lazy worker is regarded as a weakling either in mind or body, and is never held in high esteem among them.

Besides these tasks, Elizabeth often helped the Amish women when babies were born. She knew well how to care for young babies. That was why she did not hesitate to volunteer to keep five-day-old Rosanna McGonegal until her father could find a place for her among the relatives in Philadelphia. In her quiet home it was no wonder that Rosanna grew rapidly, for there was always an abundance of fresh cow's milk, fresh vegetable juices, meat broth, and everything else that could contribute to a baby's health and comfort. One day Mary Riehl, the wife of one of the ministers, came to see Elizabeth. Rosanna was lying in the cradle prattling as healthy babies often do. Mary Riehl went to the cradle to see the little Catholic baby, and when Rosanna saw her, the baby kicked and cooed happily.

Mary was so pleased that she said to Elizabeth, "Why, Lisabet, this little baby cackles chust like a little Amish baby."

Elizabeth answered in a voice of mixed joy and sadness, "Yes, sometimes I think I can hear Bridget McGonegal's voice as she prattles away trying to tell me something. I had a letter from her father the other day. He told me he has found good places for the other children and that he is working in a gravel pit near Philadelphia. As soon as he can afford it, he will come for Rosanna. My goodness, Mary, I don't know how in the world I could give her up now. I thought at first she would be a good bit of work and bother, but instead of bother she is such company for me. It seems I never get lonesome any more at all. When Pat left he said, 'Ye've been so good to me and Rosanna. May the blessed Virgin Mary comfort you and bless you every day of your life.' Mary, do you know who this Virgin Mary is?"

"Ach, them Catholics always talk about her, but I don't know who she is."

"Lisabet, I heard the other day that Cristal (Christian) Kauffman comes sneakin' over here sometimes. Is it so?"

Elizabeth lost just a little of her poise for a moment and then said disinterestedly, "Ach, why would he want to come over here anyhow now since I have this little baby to take care of?" And no more was said about that, for no Amish woman or girl of advanced years discusses her love affairs with someone else. She keeps such thoughts to herself.

"Well," said Mary, not willing to drop the subject, "I believe Cristal would make any woman a good man." Cristal Kauffman was Reuben's bachelor uncle, a man of quiet disposition and gentle manners.

But as the women went on talking Elizabeth said, "Mary, is it true that you and Jacob are thinking of moving to Lost Creek Valley with your family?"

"Yes, Lisabet, we have been thinking about it a little. You see Jacob and John Yoder are the only preachers here anymore, and neither one of them is a bishop. One of the bishops from Lost Creek Valley or Big Valley must come here whenever young people are to be baptized or married or when we have Communion. Since the congregation is getting pretty small, with so many moving away, our children would like to move some place too where there are more Amish young folks. These Catholic people here are all nice people and I like them, but they are not for our young people to run with, so maybe we'll go too sometime."

About nine o'clock one evening Rosanna was sleeping in the cradle and Elizabeth had just read a chapter in the New Testament and an evening prayer in the prayer book when she heard someone on the porch. Just then the door opened softly and who should enter but Cristal Kauffman. Elizabeth was not surprised nor was she annoyed, for Cristal always came without previous arrangement. She invited him to sit down and they began to visit. When Rosanna tossed a bit in her sleep, Elizabeth went to the cradle to fix the covers. To her surprise, Cristal came over to the cradle to see the baby.

As Rosanna lay there peacefully asleep with her

black curls and her chubby red cheeks, Cristal said, *"Mei, des is aver en sche Bopelei* (My, isn't she a pretty baby). *Ich deht so suhr gleiche es ruhm drage selver"* (I'd like to carry her around myself).

Elizabeth noticed for the first time that her heart was strangely warmed toward Cristal. Elizabeth's motherly feelings were awakened more and more and she began to love baby Rosanna very deeply.

When the long winter was over, Elizabeth was a little disturbed. At preaching service at John Yoder's it was reported that seven or eight families were moving to larger Amish settlements—some to Big Valley (Kishacoquillas), some to Buffalo Valley, and some to Lost Creek Valley. With hardly enough people left to have preaching services, she felt lonely and the need of some outside help. She remembered Mary Riehl's comment about Cristal Kauffman, "He would make any woman a good man." Mary's opinion together with Cristal's growing fondness for little Rosanna made her feel that Cristal would indeed be a great comfort.

Not long after this Cristal came to visit her again about nine o'clock in the evening and they talked of how so many families were leaving Half Moon Valley and the possibility of the congregation getting too small for preaching services and the feeling of loneliness it brought. Finally Cristal got up his courage and said gently, "Lisabet, if we would get married maybe I could help you to raise Rosanna and maybe we could get along better than we do now."

Elizabeth did not reply for some time. Then with a little smile she replied, "I think maybe you are right." And to them, that was engagement.

Since Elizabeth had no near relatives in the valley, they decided just to be married at the close of a regular preaching service, and not have a regular wedding. They set the date for spring when a bishop would have to be present anyway to officiate at the Communion service, and that would be a convenient time to be married.

The next spring Cristal and Elizabeth found that they were among the few who were still left in the Half Moon Valley congregation, so they began planning to sell the home and move to Lost Creek Valley where so many of their friends had gone.

To avoid imposing on neighbors to help haul their household goods so far, they held a sale, keeping only the essentials of housekeeping and a few articles they treasured highly. Cristal was able to put everything they still owned on his two-horse wagon, which for years he had used to haul wood and coal for the people who lived near the mines.

Although Rosanna was now nearly four years old, they thought it wise not to make the trip as long as the stormy spring weather continued, for it was a long journey, and early in the spring there might be considerable exposure.

When the May sun began to warm the earth and the farmers were busy plowing in the fields, they decided to set out for their new home—Jericho in the Lost Creek Valley of Juniata County, Pennsylvania. Early on the morning of the chosen day, several of the Amishmen still remaining in the Half Moon Valley came with their wives to help load "the flittin'." The large cookstove was heavy and the kitchen cupboard was awkward to handle. Outside of these articles, Cristal and Elizabeth could have loaded everything themselves. But among the Amish it is customary to gather for friendly helpfulness, especially when people are leaving the community or when they have some unusual task to perform where "many hands make light tasks."

When the last article was loaded, Cristal brought out

his two sorrel horses and hitched them to the wagon. Elizabeth took her place on the wagon seat, held Rosanna till Cristal took his place, then tucking Rosanna cosily between them, they waved good-bye to the friends and were off. The horses felt the crispness in the spring air and, prancing and dancing, their nimble feet sped along the smooth road just a bit too fast for comfort. Elizabeth felt a pang of sadness as she left her beloved Half Moon Valley home behind. She could not help thinking about the little party Reuben Kauffman took down this same road almost four years before. As she mused she finally said to Cristal, "Pat has never returned for the baby. I wonder why. I am sure something has happened. Will we ever know?"

Cristal said confidently, "All things work together for good to them that love the Lord," and they drove on in thoughtful silence, except when Rosanna would point to some beautiful bird, or flock of sheep, or herd of cattle.

Elizabeth and Cristal generally spoke to each other in Pennsylvania German and while Rosanna could prattle away in that language, Elizabeth was careful to teach her to speak English also. "It would be a great note if her father should come for her and she could not talk so that he could understand her," Elizabeth said.

At Bellefonte they turned right and by noon they were crossing the Seven Mountains. Here they stopped to feed their horses and eat their lunch. They took an hour off at noon, for Cristal always said, "If you want fine horses, you must take care of them." When they resumed their journey after lunch, the horses had worn off the edge of their high spirits and were content to walk instead of prance. By the time twilight shadows began to fall they had reached Reedsville, where they rested for the night.

Since there was no loading to do the second morning, by the time the sun was well up they were passing through Reed's Gap and by noon had arrived at Lewistown. They headed on into Jack's Narrows, where the Blue Juniata winds down between the mountain ranges. Progress through the Narrows was slow, and all they saw were huge oak and chestnut trees on either side of the road, mingling their branches overhead, and an occasional rabbit scampering along the road or a deer bounding up from the river bank where it had come to drink. It was twelve miles to Mifflintown where they had to go to begin the journey up through Lost Creek Valley.

By the time they reached Mifflintown, horses and people were nearly exhausted. But Cristal knew an Amish family, Jacob Hartzlers, just two miles beyond, and the road was good. On the smooth valley road the horses seemed to forget their fatigue and soon they were turning into Jacob Hartzler's barnyard for the night. When Jacob saw that they were Amish people on a journey, he gave them a warm welcome, called the boys to unhitch the horses, and graciously escorted the tired travelers to the house.

How good the cooking supper smelled to these hungry travelers, and the long table in the spacious kitchen assured them that there would be room for all. With a good night's rest, they were ready to finish the journey before noon the next day.

Joseph Yoder, who was distantly related to Cristal, lived on a large farm near Jericho. He had arranged for the house where Cristal and his family would live. When they arrived, he was on hand with a few other Amishmen and their wives. In a short time the flittin' was unloaded, everything was in its place, and dinner for all was cooking on Elizabeth's own stove.

When dinner was ready they all sat down together and bowed their heads in silent grace, thanking the Lord for food and friends and a safe journey. Even little

Rosanna seemed to bow her head longer than usual. She was taught always to bow her head and be quiet at the table before she ate.

As a young man Cristal had visited the Lost Creek Valley. Elizabeth had been here twice before—once to attend a funeral and once a wedding. But now that they were beginning their new home here, they agreed they never knew it was such a good place. The land was fertile—just rolling enough not to be swampy. The seasons were early. Best of all, many Amish people lived here with a bishop and three preachers.

Surely Lost Creek Valley was a good place to live. They were content.

CHAPTER 4

Early Education

AS May days warmed into June, they were all busy fixing up the new home. Fortunately the former owners had considerable pride in the place and had beautified it in many ways. Fine grass covered the front lawn. Morning glories twined about the trellis near the front porch. Rose bushes, lilacs and hollyhocks grew in profusion in the yard and in the garden, and the very atmosphere seemed to be scented with happiness and thrift.

Elizabeth rejoiced in all these things. Rosanna was getting old enough now to learn to work a little. Elizabeth was beginning to assign her some little responsibilities. As Elizabeth worked in the garden, Rosanna was always with her, eager to help, asking which plant was a weed and which one was a flower. As Elizabeth set out tomato or cabbage plants, she would show Rosanna and then let her try to plant one. They would

First Lesson in Gardening

remember which one Rosanna had set. Through the summer Elizabeth often called attention to how well Rosanna's plant was growing, and would praise her for being able at her age to plant something that would grow.

When Elizabeth praised her for what she had done so well, Rosanna was always so pleased that she would say, "Momly." That was Rosanna's affectionate childhood name for Elizabeth and, of course, it meant Mother. All through Rosanna's life she called Elizabeth "Momly," for there was no other name that represented so much respect and esteem and love as that name did.

Because Elizabeth was so kind to all the young people and so considerate of their wants and wishes, many of them called her Momly too. And so as they walked or worked in the garden, Rosanna would often say in her childish love for Elizabeth, "Momly, someday I can take care of the whole garden for you, and you can just sit on the porch on the rocking chair and rest yourself."

When Elizabeth was baking bread, she would always give Rosanna a little dough to knead and shape into a little loaf, or she would give her some pie dough and a little plate and have her make a little pie. In that way Rosanna learned to do the things that Amish people think are worthwhile. Elizabeth could not have qualified as a schoolteacher, but she knew child psychology intuitively. Elizabeth was always able to inspire the best in Rosanna.

In Jericho many people had horses of their own, so Cristal did not have quite so much hauling to do as he did in the Half Moon Valley. He gave more of his time to carpentering, but he still kept his two beautiful sorrels. While Rosanna was small, they continued to use Cristal's buggy to go to preaching and to go visiting. (Single men drive buggies but married men, especially after they have families, use carriages. Amish carriages are not bought on the general market; they are built to order. The church requires that carriages have a square stationary top and must be covered with white muslin or yellow oilcloth.)

One evening when Cristal came home from carpentering and while they were eating their supper, Cristal said, "Elizabeth, what would you think of us getting a new carriage to go to preaching in instead of using the buggy we now have? Rosanna is getting a little too big for you to hold on your lap when we go anywhere."

"I think it would be very nice," said Elizabeth. "Then we could take somebody with us sometimes, too. Can we afford it?"

"Oh, I think so. Do you think people would consider us proud if we put a tongue into it and drove our two horses?" asked Cristal with a little look of uncertainty.

"It might look a little stuck-up, but the people know that our horses do not like to be separated since we have only two. I don't believe they would say much about it. Besides, everybody knows that a carriage rides much better when drawn by two horses."

Pride is the cardinal sin among the Amish; so in everything they do, the possibility of being regarded as proud must be thoroughly considered. Cristal went to Mifflintown where there was a good carriage builder who built carriages for the Amish as far away as Big Valley. Cristal placed his order for a regular Amish carriage, yellow top, brown body, and black running gears and a tongue instead of shafts—a regular two-horse carriage.

The Saturday it was finally finished, Cristal took the two sorrels to bring it home. As he drove into the little barnyard, Rosanna was overjoyed to see how pretty the new carriage was. Even Elizabeth could not quite conceal her pleasure at its bright appearance. How the

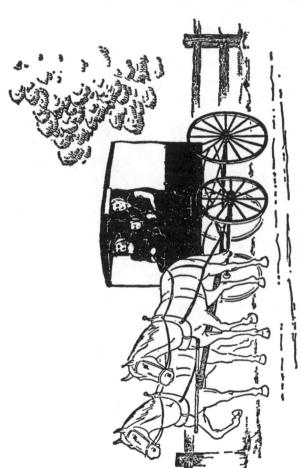

Going to Preaching in the New Carriage

wheels glistened in the sunshine. As Cristal stopped the horses, he said, "Well, what do you think?"

Elizabeth tried to look serious as she said, "It looks a little big feelin' for us, I'm afraid. But it isn't against the rules of the church to drive two horses, and everybody knows we needed a new carriage."

That evening Cristal said, "Now, you women folks get everything ready this evening; we want to go to preaching in the morning. Preaching is over at Benjamin Byler's and it is close to ten miles, so we must start a little before seven in the morning."

They were off to a good start in the morning. The full-grown corn along the way seemed to cool the air, and the horses were in fine fettle. The new carriage ran so quietly and the horses were so spirited that Cristal and Elizabeth began to analyze their own feelings to see if there might be a little pride there. It was just eight-thirty when they drove into Benjamin Byler's well kept lane.

And they were not the first to arrive. Already many white and yellow carriages stood in straight rows in the sod field just outside the barnyard. Mixed in with these were the buggies driven by the young unmarried men. Elizabeth and Rosanna alighted from the carriage and went into the house. One of the Byler boys came quickly to unhitch the horses and put them in the stable.

Cristal joined a good-sized group of men who had gathered under the "overshot" waiting until it was time to go into the house and begin the services. Cristal shook hands all around, whether he knew the men or not. Then seeing his relative, Joseph Yoder, he approached him, shook hands, and joined in the conversation. Just then Bishop Shem arrived. Two of the ministers and the deacon were already there. The bishop saluted the ministers and the deacon with the Holy Kiss and then shook hands with all the others.

In a moment the bishop said, "Well, I guess it's about time to go into the house," meaning that it was time to begin the preaching services. As Bishop Shem started for the house most of the old men followed. Soon one of the middle-aged men said, "I guess it's about time to go in," and that group went to the house. Soon all the younger men and boys followed and the house was full. While the men were taking their places, the women and girls came in and occupied the seats reserved for them.

The Amish people hold their preaching services in their houses or in the barn if the house is not large enough to accommodate the congregation, but they never hold services under trees or out in the open. The members share in turn at "taking preaching," which usually comes around about once a year. To accommodate these preaching services the Amish build their houses with movable partitions on the first floor. On preaching day all partitions can be removed and the lower part of the house becomes one big room. This makes it possible for almost everybody in the house to see and hear the preacher.

Each member provides himself with a set of benches that fit his house exactly. On preaching day these are placed properly and provide seats for the whole congregation. In one corner of this large room a table is placed and on it the hymnbooks are stacked. The hymns are all in German and the books are called *die dücke schnalle Bücher* (the thick buckle books—so called because the books are held closed by a buckle or clasp). These books contain about four hundred pages and are bound in leather.

Around this table the men singers are seated. The benches next to the table and running parallel the full length of the room are filled with other men as they come in. Next to this table, near the center of the end of the room, a bench or a row of chairs are reserved for the bishop and the ministers. The ministers face the singers' table. About two rows back of the ministers the young unmarried women sit, occupying three or four benches, and back of them the middle-aged and older women, and farthest away the mothers with babies and small children.

While the congregation is gathering, not a word is spoken. The men sit in silence with their hats on. When the house is well filled and the proper time has arrived, about 8:30 or 8:45, the deacon rises, takes some of the hymnbooks and passes them to the unmarried young women sitting just back of the men. One of the leaders of singing then announces the number of a hymn, and the men remove their hats.

As the leader begins singing and others join in, the ministers rise and withdraw to a room prepared for them upstairs. Here they engage in a short devotional exercise, attend to any church business, determine which one will "make the beginning" (preach first) and which one will preach the main sermon (*Gemeh halde*). If there is any business relative to the church or any member, it is discussed here and a course of action agreed upon. Sometimes a decision is reached to bring the matter before the whole membership.

While the bishop and the ministers are in the *Abroth* (council), the congregation continues singing hymns. The second hymn, by tradition, is always *Das Lob Sang* (Hymn of Praise). It is never announced. Amish hymns are sung in one part only and are difficult to sing. There is no written music for these hymns. Young men must learn them by rote from older singers and it frequently takes a long time. For that reason a young singer usually tries to lead this *Lob Sang* as his first attempt. He has the assurance, however, that should he get off the tune, there are older men sitting at his elbow who will take up the melody and help him along.

A third hymn is announced, but if the ministers return from the upstairs room before it is finished, the song period concludes with whatever stanza is being sung. It is not considered appropriate to sing long after the ministers return from the *Abroth* (council). As the ministers take their places again, they shake hands with all in reach who may have come in since the service began.

When the hymn is finished, the minister "making the beginning" rises and speaks for about thirty minutes. At the close of his talk the congregation kneels in silent prayer. This prayer is terminated by the bishop who stands up to indicate the close of the prayer period and the congregation rises with him. When the congregation rises, each member stands facing the bench on which he sat, while the deacon reads a chapter from the New Testament (never from the Old Testament).

After the reading the congregation is seated and the minister who will preach the sermon stands up. He frequently preaches for an hour and a half and on special occasions for two hours. All this time the people are seated on backless benches, demonstrating endurance as well as devotion. Soon after the main speaker has begun his discourse, the hostess comes in quietly carrying a platter filled with good-sized pieces of half-moon pies. She gives a piece to each child in the room, for by this time the children are getting a little hungry and restless.

When the main speaker has finished the first part of his sermon, he is seated. He then calls on each minister and deacon present for a testimony or an additional thought, if they wish to give it. If a respected visiting Amishman is present, the speaker may call on him for a testimony whether he is a minister or not.

After the testimonies the main speaker rises again and expresses gratitude that his discourse was considered orthodox. After a few brief remarks, the congregation again kneels in prayer while the preacher reads aloud from the prayerbook. The same prayer is always used (the Amish never offer original prayers anywhere). When this prayer is ended, they all stand again facing the bench on which they sat as before, while the minister pronounces the benediction. As he closes the benediction with the words, *"Durch Jesum Christum, Amen"* (Through Jesus Christ, Amen), the whole congregation bow perceptibly at the knee and are seated.

At this point the deacon makes all the announcements, publishes the names of those intending to marry soon, and then requests the members to remain seated if there is any church business (the others are excused). Following the other announcements, he names the home where preaching will be held in two weeks. When he is through, some man at the singers' table announces the number of a hymn. When the last note of the hymn has died away, the men rise slowly, put on their hats, and slowly pass out of the house. As the men file out, the young women begin leaving and then the older ones. The women either go outside or to some other part of the house.

As soon as the room is empty, the man of the house and his helpers remove all the benches except a few retained for tables and seats. Then at the most convenient place, usually through the longest part of the house, two tables are set up made of two benches set side by side— one table for men and one for women.

Girls who have volunteered to help the hostess come quickly, spread white table cloths over these bench tables and set them. First a knife, a spoon, a cup and saucer, and a drinking glass are placed along each side of the table about two feet apart. Then large plates of bread, half-moon pies (dried apple pies), green apple pies, butter, apple butter, cream, red beets, and pickles are placed on the table. To this are added large bowls of hot bean soup. This is the standard preaching meal, and it never varies.

When all is ready, the man of the house goes to the door and announces, "Dinner is ready." The bishop, the ministers, the deacon, and the old men go in first until the table is full. While the men are taking their places, the old and middle-aged women are being seated at their table. When both tables are filled, the host announces, "The tables are full," whereupon the bishop says, "Let us pray." All bow their heads and engage in silent prayer. No audible blessing is ever uttered. When grace is over, the girls who set the tables come with large pots of hot coffee, offering coffee to all who wish it. These girls then wait on the tables, replenishing bread plates and pie plates and offering second helpings of coffee to all.

When everyone has finished eating, a brief pause is observed and then the bishop says, "If we are all through, let us give thanks," and a silent prayer of thanksgiving follows. When this prayer is over, both men and women arise from the tables and leave the room. The waitresses come and reset the tables, but they do not wash the dishes.

When the tables are ready the second time, the man of the house again goes to the door and announces that dinner is ready. The older men who have not eaten yet and the middle-aged men fill the one table, and the older women and the middle-aged women fill the table for the women. When the places are all taken, the man of the house announces again that the table is full, and without any word from the bishop or anyone else, they all bow their heads in silent grace. In the same way table after table is served and replenished, being filled each time with younger persons, until finally the little boys and girls who can care for themselves fill the table. Younger children go to the table with their parents. Finally when all have eaten, everything is cleared away.

The house wife never needs to worry about what she will serve for dinner; the meal is always the same. And there is a regular form of preparation. On the Wednesday prior to preaching services a half dozen women of the same church come and help polish the tinware. On Friday three or four come to help bake the bread, as many as forty big loaves. On Saturday a dozen women come to help bake about sixty green apple pies and four or five hundred half-moon pies. The latter are made of dried apples cooked to about the consistency of apple sauce. A piece of pie dough is then rolled out to the thickness of pie crust, circular in shape. The dried apples are spread on one half of it and the other half is brought over the apples and pinched tight at the edges, making a pie the form of a half circle or half moon. These are laid on tin pie plates and baked. Since they are all of one piece with the edges tightly pinched together, they are easily served.

It usually takes from about one o'clock to three to serve a Sunday dinner. While one group is eating, the other men stand around the barn or in the yard and visit. The topic of conversation is usually crops, weather, markets, cattle, and sometimes religion. While the men chat outside, the women visit in the house. They generally talk about gardens, housecleaning, chickens, butter making, or some moral question. Sometimes a little gossip slips in. In this way Amish preaching serves two purposes, religious guidance and a social occasion.

About three o'clock, or sooner, if the family has all had dinner, the husband goes to the house or sends a little boy to see whether mother is ready to go home. From about 2:30 on, long rows of white and yellow carriages move silently out the lane, until the field where they were parked is again empty and preaching is over.

On this particular Sunday as Cristal drove up to the gate for Elizabeth and Rosanna with his two prancing sorrels, the bishop happened to be there, too. Looking at Cristal's shiny carriage and prancing horses he said good-naturedly, "Be a little careful, Cristal. This looks pretty high toned."

Cristal laughed and replied, "Well, a carriage has to be new once, you know."

"Jah, well," said Bishop Shem, which in modern language means "O. K."

As they drove home, Elizabeth sighed with relief as she said to Cristal, "Well, if the bishop didn't scold about our two-horse carriage, I guess it's all right."

Just then little Rosanna spoke up and said, "Cristal, did you notice? We had the nicest carriage at preaching today."

Elizabeth felt it her duty to say, "Tut, tut, Rosanna, you must not talk that way. We must not be proud."

A little later in the fall when the chestnut burrs began to crack open, Rosanna was old enough to start to school. Fortunately, the schoolhouse was not far away and there was a good lady teacher, all of which relieved Elizabeth greatly. She had been talking to Rosanna about school and how nice it would be to learn new things with the other children.

Rosanna's eyes sparkled with the idea of going to school. Her wavy hair had a glossy luster, her bright eyes sparkled more and more, and her cheeks took on a rosy red that assured Elizabeth that Rosanna was in perfect health.

When Rosanna left for school that first morning, Elizabeth stood watching until she had almost reached the schoolhouse. Elizabeth was not emotional, but this morning she had great trouble in restraining her tears, and in her heart she prayed, "O Lord, let nothing happen to this dear little motherless girl whom Thou hast given me to raise. Guard Rosanna from all harm that she may grow up and glorify Thy name."

It was the first day in over six years that Rosanna was away from Elizabeth. All day Elizabeth felt that there was a dreadful emptiness in the house and a painful fullness in her heart. Rosanna too felt that it was a long day, sitting there on a bench and not being able to talk to Momly; so when school was out, she took her little dinner pail and hurried home as fast as she could go.

As the afternoon wore on, Elizabeth could not help but keep looking down the road to see whether Rosanna was coming, and when she finally saw her in her little blue dress, long black apron, and little white cap, come skipping up the road, her heart swelled with joy. She never realized before just how much Rosanna really did mean to her.

That evening at the supper table Rosanna told Cristal and Elizabeth all that had happened at school that day. The teacher, Mary McLaughlin, had called her a smart little girl, and Rosanna liked her for that, for she did want to be smart. She was glad that she could say almost all of the ABC's the very first day. Before going to bed she had Cristal go over them once more with her.

Mary McLaughlin liked Rosanna and Rosanna liked Mary McLaughlin. Occasionally Elizabeth would send a rose or an apple or a cookie to school with Rosanna for the teacher. Elizabeth wanted Mary McLaughlin to know that she had a high regard for her. Besides it was a good way to teach Rosanna to be thoughtful and considerate of others. On the way home from school Mary McLaughlin would sometimes stop and talk to Elizabeth, mentioning how well Rosanna was getting along

Returning from First Day at School

with her studies and how well-behaved she was. And all this seemed to fulfill Elizabeth's prayers.

Year after year followed pleasantly. But Cristal developed a bad heart condition. Gradually he became worse, and finally he died.

One evening when they were alone and very lonely Elizabeth said, "Rosanna, we never know what will happen. You may have to make your own living someday. You get along so well in school that I have been thinking it might be wise for you to get ready to teach school. That pays better than lots of jobs. Besides it's much nicer work. Do you think you would like to be a schoolteacher, Rosanna?"

"Oh, yes, Momly. That way I could earn money for you, too, if you ever need it."

The Amish people as a rule are opposed to education beyond the "three R's," quoting the Bible, *"Die Weisheit dieser Weld ist ein Greil vor Gott"* (The wisdom of this world is foolishness before God). For Elizabeth to decide deliberately to train her little orphan girl to be a teacher took genuine courage.

CHAPTER 5

Finding Little Sister

ROSANNA'S older sister, Margaret, and her brothers, John and William, were taken to Philadelphia, as mentioned before, and good homes were found for them among friends and relatives. Being considerably older than Rosanna, they had by this time almost grown up. Margaret favored the O'Connors and became a tall, stately woman. William, the older of the boys, was very ambitious and as soon as he was old enough secured a position in a store in Philadelphia. He and John Wanamaker, of later department store fame, clerked together as young men in the same store. John, the younger brother, was smaller and less rugged. John learned to be a typesetter and worked for the *Philadelphia Public Ledger* all his life.

William, the older of the boys, assumed responsibility for the family after his father, Pat, was killed in an accident. He was old enough to remember how Reuben Kauffman, the young Amishman, had brought them to Bellefonte to the railroad station, and how he refused to accept any pay for this service saying, "We Amish like to help our neighbors, but not for pay." He distinctly remembered that Reuben had long hair, wore a broadbrimmed hat and hooks and eyes on his coat and vest. He knew that other plain sects wear long hair and broad hats, but the Amish are the only ones with hooks and eyes on their coats and vests. This knowledge was useful to William as he clerked in the general store. He had no trouble recognizing Amishmen as they came to buy and trade. He also remembered that somewhere among the Amish his little sister Rosanna was being brought up.

In those days farmers from Centre, Mifflin, and Juniata counties hauled their grain to Philadelphia in large Conestoga wagons drawn by four or six horses or mules. After marketing their grain, they would go into the stores to buy groceries and dry goods for the year. William McGonegal decided that he would try to find his sister, Rosanna. He felt sure that someday an Amish farmer would come into the store who knew Rosanna.

Whenever a man came into the store wearing hooks and eyes on his coat and vest, William would step up to him and say, "Pardon me, neighbor, but do you by any chance know a little girl named Rosanna McGonegal?"

He asked this question to scores of Amishmen for two or three years and they all looked at him soberly for a moment and then said, "No, I never saw her." It was discouraging when so many said "No," but he felt confident that someday he would find the right man.

One day Joseph Yoder of the Lost Creek Valley took a load of grain to Philadelphia and went into this store to buy his groceries. Joseph Yoder was a short, stocky man with long hair, a well-kept beard, an honest face, and a pleasant disposition. When there was a good opportunity William stepped up to Joseph and said, "Pardon me, neighbor, but do you by chance know a little girl named Rosanna McGonegal?"

Joseph look at him and smiling said, "Yes, I know her well."

"I'm William McGonegal, her oldest brother," William informed him excitedly. "Would you be kind enough to tell me how I could find her?"

"She lives in Jericho and is being raised by Elizabeth Kauffman."

William was overjoyed. He remembered that Elizabeth Yoder, an unmarried woman, had agreed to keep Rosanna till his father should come for her. Surely this was the woman and this was his little sister.

"How can I go there?" said William.

"Take a train to Thompsontown. Then take a stagecoach for Jericho and ask for Mrs. Cristal Kauffman. Anybody there can tell you where she lives."

When Joseph returned from his long journey to Philadelphia, he went over and told Elizabeth how he had seen William McGonegal, and how William had asked about Rosanna and the way to come here. "So," Joseph said, "I suppose this young man will come to see you someday. He's a fine looking young fellow and he's very polite."

"Jah, well," said Elizabeth, resignedly, sensing a little

danger of losing Rosanna, "if he comes, I guess we can keep him."

That evening when the store closed William hurried over to see his sister Margaret to tell her the glorious news. William threw his arms about her, kissed her and exclaimed, "O Margaret, I have the most wonderful news. I have found Rosanna. For years I have been asking Amishmen whether they ever saw Rosanna and they all said 'No.' But today a fine looking Amishman came into the store, and when I asked him whether he knew a little girl named Rosanna McGonegal he said, 'Yes, I know her well.' She is now living in Jericho and he told me how to get there."

Margaret could hardly find words to express her joy. Then she said to William, "Perhaps you can bring her here, and we can have her baptized and confirmed in the Catholic Church."

"I'll go just as soon as the spring rush is over and I'll bring her here if it is at all possible. Of course, Margaret, the Amish are a mighty fine religious people and I cannot help but believe that she is all right with them, but it would be so nice to have her here and go to church with us. I'm so anxious to see how she looks. Do you think the lady who took her is dressing her Amish?"

One morning early in July, William McGonegal bought a ticket on the Pennsylvania Railroad for Thompsontown. William had never traveled far from the city before, but he felt equal to the occasion. As he left the Atlantic plain about Philadelphia and approached the foothills of the Alleghenies, the mountains, the ravines and river valleys, his memory brought back vividly the scenes of his boyhood in the Half Moon Valley. He remembered again the railroad station at Bellefonte and half wished his journey was taking him there.

When the train finally stopped at Thompsontown, about four o'clock in the afternoon, he got off and began looking for a stagecoach. Presently he saw what he supposed was a stagecoach—two horses hitched to a good-sized covered wagon. Seeing the driver, a big husky fellow, approaching, William asked, "Is this the stagecoach for Jericho?"

"Yes, sir, my boy," said the driver accommodatingly.

"Could you take me there and let me off near the house of Mrs. Cristal Kauffman?"

"Yes, sir, my boy. Step right in."

"Could you tell me whether a little girl lives there named Rosanna McGonegal?"

"Yes, sir, my boy. And she's just about the smartest little girl in the community. She's a friend to everybody and everybody is her friend," said the driver in a reassuring way.

The stagecoach jolted William every time it hit a rough spot in the road, but in his anxiety to see Rosanna it did not go half fast enough.

Elizabeth did not know on which day William was coming; so she had not made any special preparation. But there always was plenty of good fresh milk in the cellar, eggs in the basket, hams in the smokehouse, and a supply of bread and pies in the cupboard, so she could set a good meal at a moment's notice, any time.

When William arrived, he knocked on the front door. He heard a pleasant voice say, "Come in." He had expected someone to come to the door but as no one did, he opened the door softly and found Elizabeth and Rosanna in the living room. As William looked at this tall muscular woman, he thought he recalled Elizabeth Yoder of Half Moon Valley, and he said, "Is this Elizabeth Kauffman?" William remembered that Amish people are not much for titles, so he didn't address her as Mrs. Kauffman.

"Yes," said Elizabeth quietly.

"I am William McGonegal, and is this little girl my sister, Rosanna?"

"Yes, that is Rosanna McGonegal. I have never changed her name because your father said he would come for her sometime, and I thought he could find her easier if I did not change her name. Is your father still living?"

"No," said William, "he was killed. After taking us children to Philadelphia, he worked in a gravel pit to earn money to clothe us children and someday come for Rosanna. While at work one day, the pit caved in. Three men were killed, just covered up with tons and tons of rock and gravel, and father was one of them. He was so anxious to come for Rosanna so he could have us all together."

Elizabeth was silent for a moment. Then in a voice filled with deep sympathy she said, "I knew something had happened. When we moved out of Half Moon Valley I said to Cristal, my husband, I know something has happened to Patrick McGonegal. He had written me a letter not long before saying that he was working in a gravel pit and hoped to come for Rosanna as soon as he could earn enough money to make the trip. Now I know why he never came."

Although Rosanna was nine years old, she was a little wary of this stranger. He did not have long hair and a beard like Cristal had, and he did not wear hooks and eyes on his coat and vest. And his hands were softer and whiter than Momly's hands and his clothes were so smooth. "Such a different looking man," thought Rosanna to herself as she stood close to Elizabeth's chair.

After they had talked a few minutes, Momly said, "You haven't had any supper yet, have you?"

"No," said William. "I'm not usually a heavy eater,

but I must confess that stagecoach ride has made me rather hungry."

Momly left the room and in a surprisingly short time announced, "Supper is ready. Just come out here to the kitchen. It's only a light meal. Would you like to wash before you eat?" When William said he would, Momly filled the basin with warm water, placed it on a near-by bench, laid a piece of soap beside it, hung a fresh towel on a nail and said, "You can wash here." William was not accustomed to washing in the kitchen, but knowing that Amish people do not have bathrooms, he conformed gracefully.

When William sat down to the table, he was amazed at what Momly had prepared in so short a time—luscious thick slices of chestnut brown fried ham, three fried eggs with golden yellow yolks, fried potatoes flavored with onion, stewed tomatoes, red beets and pickles, homemade bread, butter yellow as gold, apple butter and quince jelly, and for a final course, a piece of cherry pie cut from the largest pie William had ever seen.

"Will you drink coffee or milk? You are welcome to both if you care for them."

"This supper is so good," said William, "that I think I can't refuse either of them, so I'll take both."

When he had eaten all he could hold Momly said, "Take some more. You've had a long ride."

"I have eaten more already than I usually do, but everything was so good and I was so hungry, I just couldn't quit, Momly. (William had heard Rosanna call Elizabeth 'Momly'; so to make her feel free with him he also called her Momly.) If this is just a light meal, I would like to be here sometime when you prepare a regular meal. I don't believe it could be better than this one was."

Momly never responded to anything that sounded

like flattery, so she simply said, "I hope you had enough to eat."

William tried to make friends with Rosanna, but his smart clothes and his unusual interest in her seemed to put her on her guard. Trying to explain to her that he was her brother and that his name was McGonegal, too, didn't seem to help. How could he be her brother? He was not Momly's son and she certainly was Momly's little girl. Not until Rosanna was thirteen years old did she come to understand that Momly was not her real mother. When she did, she wept broken-heartedly for two days.

Next day Rosanna agreed to take William out to the garden to see the flowers, and the vegetables she had planted. She also took him down to the school-house where Mary McLaughlin had taught her for the last four winters. Forgetting her reserve for a moment, Rosanna said, "When I get big, Momly wants me to be a schoolteacher and I want to be one too. Then I can earn lots of money and I can help Momly, if she needs anything."

William had hoped to take Rosanna back to Philadelphia with him, but he could not help but rejoice in the loyalty she showed toward Elizabeth.

When William went to bed that night, he noticed that there was no carpet on the floor, no pictures on the walls, no curtains on the windows, and no wash-bowl in the room. Everything was severely plain, but immaculately clean. The bed was high and the mattress was filled with finely cut straw. But when once his tired body nestled down into that crude mattress, he thought he never rested more comfortably. Before he drifted off into sleep, he could not help but ponder the simple, efficient life of this plain woman. The words "quiet simplicity, peace, and contentment" again and again floated through his mind. What a supper; what cleanliness; what piety; what freedom from strife and rivalry; and what joy and gladness Rosanna showed in obeying Elizabeth's every wish.

As sleep approached, his mind drifted back to Half Moon Valley. Again he heard his father say to Elizabeth as he left little eight-day-old Rosanna with her, "Elizabeth, it's bin mighty fine and good of ye to help me so, and I'll never stop askin' the Virgin Mary to bless you and the baby and shield you from harm and want," and surely that prayer was answered. As the mountains of Half Moon Valley closed in upon him and shut out the light, he fell slowly into a restful sleep.

The next afternoon William asked what had been weighing heavily on his mind. "Elizabeth, will you let me take Rosanna back to Philadelphia with me and make a little Catholic girl out of her?"

Elizabeth had sensed from the beginning that this was why William had come. She was silent for a long moment and then said in a voice almost breaking with sadness, "No, Rosanna is the only little girl I have. I have taken care of her ever since she was five days old and I could not give her up now."

At this Rosanna spoke up with her usual Irish quickness and said, "And I would not go with you either. I would not leave my mother."

When William saw that he could not persuade Elizabeth to give her up, he said, "Well, then just let her go along with me to the station on the stagecoach tomorrow."

But Elizabeth's quick intuition warned her of his intentions. "Oh, no, it is too far for such a little girl to go on the stage," she replied.

But William kept insisting that she go along. As the Amish people practice the Biblical injunction, "Be yet easily entreated," Elizabeth felt she had no other choice but to let Rosanna go with him. But she took a precaution that she felt would work. She knew how everyone took an interest in Rosanna as a little orphan girl, and how they all loved her for her witty sayings and her friendship for everybody: Elizabeth was confident that if she confided in big John Young, the stage driver, she could arrange things all right.

That evening after supper while Rosanna and William were washing the dishes, she walked over to see big John. He was busy lubricating the axles of the stagecoach. John looked up and said, "Why, good evening, Elizabeth. What can I do for you this evening?"

"Much," said Elizabeth.

Then she told him how Rosanna's brother was visiting there, how he had pled to take Rosanna back to Philadelphia with him and make a little Catholic girl out of her, and how she had refused to give her up. She explained that William was begging her to allow Rosanna to go along to the station with him in the morning, and that she had grave misgivings that he intended to take her with him by force.

"You see, John, I almost had to allow her to go to the station with him because he insisted so hard. But when I gave my consent, I felt that I could depend on you to look after her and see that he does not take her." Big John straightened up to his full height, took off his hat and said, "Elizabeth, go home and don't worry a minute. If he takes her, he'll do it over my dead body. We'll never let anyone steal our little girl."

Next morning when the stage arrived, William and Rosanna were ready to go. When they were safely seated, big John gave Elizabeth a knowing look, cracked the whip, and the two slick-coated black horses whisked them away in a cloud of dust.

When they arrived at the station in Thompsontown, big John tied his horses to the nearest hitching pole. Then he came over to where Rosanna stood, took her hand in his, and looked at the slick slender city boy as much as to say, "Now, smarty, just you touch this little girl to take her with you by force, and I'll tie your slender body into knots." William saw through it all in a minute, and he did not even ask Rosanna to get on the train with him.

Big John and Rosanna stood watching the train speed away till it was lost around the curve in the river, then walked to the stagecoach. Big John lifted Rosanna into the coach and said, "Little girl, you do not know what I did for you today." On the way back to Jericho the thought of that young fellow kidnapping Rosanna made big John so angry that he clenched his huge fist and said, "By the eternals, if that smarty had touched this little girl, I'd a punched the daylights out of him." He swelled with pride as he thought of the confidence Elizabeth had placed in him.

When Rosanna came running into the house, Elizabeth said, "Was it a nice ride?"

"Oh, yes, and at the station big John stood beside me and held my hand. Momly, why did he do that?"

"Maybe he thought William might take you along, if he didn't take care of you."

"I thought of that, too. But when big John held my hand in his I wasn't a bit afraid."

William went back to Philadelphia with a glowing report of Rosanna's brilliancy and beauty. "Does Elizabeth dress her in Amish clothes?" asked Margaret.

"Yes, she does, and with her little black apron and her little black bonnet she looks as pretty as a little nun. Why, the beauty of the shamrock is in her grace, the roses of Killarney in her cheeks, the sparkle of her waters in her eyes and Saint Cecilia's own music in her voice," he said, using almost the very words their father had spoken about their mother many years before. But his scheme to bring Rosanna back with him had not worked. It was thwarted by an untrained woman with a keen mind and simple faith in God.

CHAPTER 6

The Kishacoquillas

AS the seasons came and went the people around Jericho became more and more friendly to the quiet widow and her little Irish charge. It seemed everyone took an interest in Rosanna as though they too had been appointed by Providence to help bring her up. When Elizabeth took her along to the village store, Mr. Banks would ask her questions about the garden or about school just to see her enthusiasm. To see her black eyes sparkle, all one needed to do was to say something disparagingly about Mary McLaughlin, the schoolteacher, and Rosanna defended her staunchly.

Elizabeth and Rosanna lived happily in Lost Creek Valley where the orchards and gardens and fields and cattle all suggested peace and plenty. However, they did miss Cristal, and the two beautiful sorrel horses they had to sell after he died. As they discussed their loneliness for Cristal, they talked more and more about Rosanna studying to be a teacher. If she continued to make such fine progress in school, it would be only a few years until she could take the county examination, get a certificate, and teach.

"But what will we do about your dress?" said Elizabeth. "There are no Amish girls who teach school. Maybe they will laugh at your plain dress and cap."

"Well," said Rosanna, "I'll be such a good teacher

that they will not think about my clothes. Besides, I might be able to get the Renno School and there the pupils are nearly all Amish." It was a fine idea, and they looked forward together to the day when Rosanna would be a teacher.

As harvesttime approached, Rosanna said, "Momly, would you let me go over to Joseph Yoder's to help in the harvest field, if they need me? I could earn some money, and then I could buy some of my own clothes and that would save some for you."

"Do you think you are strong enough to work in the field?"

"Well, I'm not very big but I believe I can do more work than Joseph's girls can, and they help sometimes."

"Jah, well," said Elizabeth agreeing somewhat reluctantly.

The next time Rosanna saw Joseph Yoder in the village, she said to him, "Good morning, Joseph. I'd like to help you in the harvest. Do you need any help?"

"Well, now, let me see," parried Joseph. "Do you think you could carry sheaves or heap hay?"

"Of course I can. And I can build wheat sheaves too, I believe."

"Well, you're pretty spunky. I'll let you try. I'll send for you when the hay is ready to haul."

Rosanna could hardly wait till she reached home to tell Momly that she was going to help Joseph Yoder make hay and harvest. For the first time she would have some money that she had earned herself, and that would be something to look forward to.

When haymaking time came, she found that she could heap hay almost as fast as the men, and she could turn sheaves for the man who did the mowing. Some of the other jobs she could not handle as well as the men, but she worked hard. When she had helped ten days in all, and Joseph paid her thirty-five cents per day, she was delighted.

"Momly, just think. I have three dollars and a half, and I'm going to save it, too." (All Amish children are taught to earn money if they can and save it for a useful purpose. To the credit of the Amish people none of them ever accept welfare payments of any kind. They may not make much money, but they try to save part of all they earn.)

A year or so before Cristal Kauffman passed away, Sarah, the wife of Bishop Shem Yoder, died. Shem had two sons, Sam and Yost, and one daughter, Leah. Yost, the oldest of the children, was already married and had a home of his own. By hiring someone to do most of the work, and by some of the relatives coming in to help sometimes, the Bishop got along reasonably well. But it was not real housekeeping, Shem observed. He was also concerned that Leah was not being taught to work as a young girl should be. A bishop had to set a good example for the congregation, so Shem Yoder had showed no outward signs until now that he was interested in finding another. According to the scriptures, however, a bishop should have a wife and a family of well-instructed, obedient children.

Since Sarah had been gone for almost three years now, Shem felt that no one could criticize him if he decided to marry again. There were not many women available. It would not look right for him to marry a young woman. He knew a few middle-aged unmarried women, but because of the very fact that they were unmarried he did not care to consider them. As he pondered the problem he found that the most suitable woman in the congregation for a bishop's wife was Elizabeth Kauffman, Cristal Kauffman's widow. She was a good worker, had a quiet dispostion, was devout and dressed strictly according to the rules of the church. There was only one slight drawback—the half-grown Irish girl she was raising. How would Leah and Sam get along with her? He knew that Rosanna was smart in school, a good worker and quick-witted, while Leah was much less gifted. He had trouble keeping Sam in school till he mastered the "three R's." He knew, too, that Elizabeth simply adored Rosanna. If he married Elizabeth, it would take some fine diplomacy to keep things running smoothly.

One day when he had some business in the village, the bishop stopped to see Elizabeth on the pretext of finding out whether Rosanna wasn't about old enough to join the church. He found Elizabeth cordial and rather quiet, and as for the little Irish girl, she was so pleasant to the bishop that he could not help but like her. She seemed so helpful and friendly. She was already taking over some of the responsibilities of the house so that Elizabeth would have fewer cares. Nothing could please the bishop more; that was Christian education and he did not even try to conceal his pleasure.

On the way home, a new concern arose. Why Rosanna is much more considerate of Elizabeth than Leah and Sam are of me, he mused. If Elizabeth and I should marry, and she were as kind to me as she is to Elizabeth, I am afraid I would like her better than my own children. *"Immer Druwel ergitz"* (Always trouble somewhere).

He felt that his visit had gone well. He had inquired about Rosanna joining the church, whether Elizabeth had plenty of firewood for the winter, and whether she had much trouble in finding a way to go to preaching. But he was uncertain whether he showed too much approval of Rosanna and whether he had entirely concealed his admiration for Elizabeth. *"Well, wass machts aus"* (Well, what does it matter); if people talk, let them talk. He would pray over the matter and try to follow God's leading.

The next Sunday at preaching his full round cheeks became a little redder as Rosanna came to him and said, "Bishop Shem, Momly and I have been talking about my joining church this summer and Momly thinks I am still a little too young, so I will wait a year or two yet."

"Jah, well," said Shem just a little embarrassed, "but you will not put it off too long, will you?"

"Oh, no. I'll join just as soon as I am big enough." Shem noticed that a few men heard what Rosanna had said. From their conversation they could easily conclude that he had been over to Elizabeth's house. He was aware, too, how little it takes to start rumors flying about a widower and a widow. He tried hard to make it appear that he was simply attending to the duties of the bishopric.

As autumn approached, Shem saw clearly that his household was not being well run. Leah was young. Although she tried hard, she did not accomplish everything that needed to be done. There was very little canned fruit in the cellar, very few dried apples and tomatoes, and no dried corn. It was time to cook apple butter and soap and there was nobody to go ahead with it.

As he prayed for guidance, the leading seemed clearly toward Elizabeth Kauffman. But he must not be hasty. Whenever there was a real reason to talk to Elizabeth he never lost an opportunity. The more he saw of her and Rosanna the better he liked both of them.

When the autumn days were deepening into winter and the young Amish folks were being "published" (having their marriage announced in church), Shem felt that the time was right. He went over to David Renno, one of the ministers under him, laid the matter confidently before him, and asked his advice. After thinking through the situation, David expressed entire approval. Shem said, "If you approve, Brother David, then I choose you to be my *Schteckleimann.* Do your duty."

David's duty then was, according to Amish custom, to go by night without anyone knowing it, call on Elizabeth, mention Shem's desire to marry her, and receive her reply.

David waited until he was sure Rosanna would be asleep. When he was seated he said, "I have come at the request of Bishop Shem to ask you to consider being his wife." He gently called attention to her widowhood and her need of both moral and financial support. Shem Yoder was the bishop of the church, well thought of by both congregations, and even by other denominations, and was well-to-do. Since Sarah passed away, David explained, Bishop Shem needed someone with character and experience, who was in good standing in the church, to help him raise his family. "And," David concluded modestly, "I think, Sister Elizabeth, that you would suit the place better than anybody else in the church. What answer may I take back to Shem?"

This visit from David Renno was not entirely unexpected to Elizabeth. She had been noticing the bishop's friendliness to Rosanna and her. Intuition told her unmistakably that Shem Yoder was interested in her. She remained silent for a few moments. Then she said, "If the bishop wishes it that way, I will try to do my part."

The next day David Renno went over to see the bishop, who was obviously very anxious to know the answer. When David told the Bishop that he had fulfilled the duties of his office, but he teased just a little by withholding the answer for a moment. Then he said, "Elizabeth agrees that if marriage is your wish, she will try to do her part."

"Thank God," said the bishop, "and thank you, Brother David, for interceding for me."

After a brief wedding ceremony, Elizabeth and Rosanna moved to Shem Yoder's big house to become part of his family. Elizabeth's experienced eye saw many things for the women of the house to do. Her own house, although plainly furnished, had been kept immaculate. Here windows needed washing, floors needed scrubbing, the tinware was unpolished, the stove had lost its luster, and there were no flowers in the house or in the yard.

Rosanna found that helping to milk, looking after the chickens and eggs, and carrying skimmed milk to the pigs gave her more to do than when they lived in the village. But when there was work to be done, she did it uncomplainingly.

Bishop Shem had just returned from Big Valley where he had gone to help hold a communion service. Besides being interested in the growing congregation there, he was greatly impressed with the fertility of the land and the unmistakable signs of prosperity. He explained this to Elizabeth and asked whether she would be willing to move to Big Valley (Kishacoquillas Valley) if he could buy a good farm there. When Elizabeth saw his enthusiasm, she simply said in her quiet way, *"Jah, well,"* meaning, I am not greatly interested but I am willing to do as you wish. What he did not tell her at once was that he had already spotted a farm for sale that appealed to him. This farm lay just north of Belleville, a thriving little town in the heart of the Kishacoquillas Valley. It was part of a tract of two thousand acres granted by the William Penn Estate to Capt. John Armstrong for his services in the French and Indian War. While the Amish are not greatly interested in historic facts, nevertheless, Bishop Shem rather liked the idea of owning a farm so closely connected with the history of the country.

Bishop Shem made it a point to go to the valley soon to see whether he could buy the farm. He had no trouble arranging the purchase and getting a clear title and deed. When he returned to Lost Creek Valley this time, anybody could see that there was a new joy and inspiration in his heart. He was moving to Big Valley soon, where there were large congregations of Amish people living.

Early the next spring Bishop Shem asked a few of his members to bring their teams and help him move to the valley. They loaded all the wagons in the evening so that the bishop and his family could get an early start the next day. The bishop had a two-horse team and a four-horse team of his own. With the help of a few of the members they had no trouble getting all the household goods and the farm implements on the wagons.

Next morning before daybreak a caravan of five horse-drawn wagons started on the long journey to Kishacoquillas Valley. More than half the trip was over the same road that Cristal, Elizabeth, and Rosanna had come some ten years before. At Reedsville where they stayed overnight on their first journey, however, they turned to the left. A new road led into the beautiful Kishacoquillas, to new friends and a new home.

The prospect of a larger church, more young folks and greater prosperity pleased Rosanna, but the pleasure was slightly dimmed by the thought of leaving her good friends in Lost Creek Valley. However, the farm which the bishop bought could not have been better chosen so far as Rosanna's future joy and happiness were concerned.

CHAPTER 7

New Friends

THE women busily arranged the furniture in the new home while the men placed the farming implements in the barn. Elizabeth and Rosanna were pleased with the new house. It was a large house with a high porch running all the way along the front. On the ground floor was a cool basement to be used as kitchen in hot weather, with two small rooms for storing canned fruits and vegetables. Large bins of apples would make winter months a delight.

On the second floor was a large kitchen, a dining room (although most of the eating would be done in the kitchen), a large living room, and a bedroom. All the walls were movable so that when they had preaching the first floor could be converted into one large room, and and everyone could see and hear the preacher. Upstairs were five large bedrooms, assuring them adequate room to house visitors.

Besides a large bank barn, there were all the necessary outbuildings. This farm was complete in every detail. There was plenty of stable room for Bishop Shem's six horses, eight or ten cows, a dozen steers, and a flock of sheep. The upper part of the barn was divided into four large mows, two of which were used as threshing floors. These floors were so well laid that, if occasion demanded, they could be swept and used for preaching services or for a "barn-party" when the young folks gathered for an evening of party plays and singing.

The farm, being rather large, required lots of work and long hours. During the summer months everybody

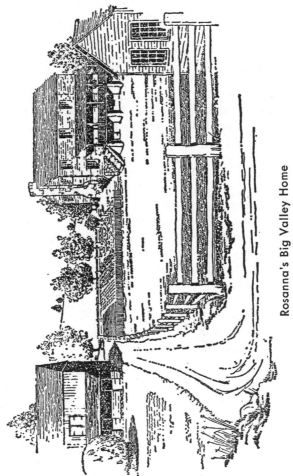

Rosanna's Big Valley Home

arose at five o'clock. Amish bishops and ministers do not receive any pay for their services, so Bishop Shem rose with the rest. He usually fed the horses and the cows while Sam, his son, curried the horses and harnessed them for the field.

While the men were doing their morning chores, Elizabeth built the fire in the kitchen stove and prepared breakfast. Rosanna and Leah went to the barn and milked the cows. By the time Shem had the horses and cows fed, Sam had the horses harnessed and ready for the field, the girls had the milking done, and Elizabeth had breakfast ready. Then they all gathered in the kitchen at the table and bowed their heads in silent grace. Amish people never engage in audible grace and rarely have family worship, but at the close of each meal they observe a silent prayer of thanksgiving. In an Amish family, everybody must be at the table on time and must remain at the table till the silent prayer of thanksgiving is over. To leave the table before the last silent thanks is observed would be a violation of a religious observance.

Elizabeth had been a good mother to Rosanna and now she wanted to be a good mother to Leah, too. Elizabeth would let one of the girls wash the dishes while she and the other one made the beds, did the sweeping, cleaned the yard or worked in the garden. Shem could easily see that Rosanna was much better trained to work than Leah was, so he said to Elizabeth, *"Now, mach sie schaffe"* (Now, make her work). The Bishop's own daughter certainly did not dare stigmatize the family by being a poor worker. Elizabeth spent a lot of time with Leah trying to teach her better working habits. When Rosanna showed some impatience with Leah and complained to Elizabeth that Leah was so slow, Elizabeth would say in her kind patient way, "You see, Rosanna, Leah did not have an Irish mother that was quick like you did, so you must just be glad and patient. She'll learn someday."

"Yes, Momly, you're right; I know."

One of Rosanna's great concerns was the kind of school they had at Belleville. One day at the dinner table she mentioned that she could hardly wait for school to start. Turning to Sam she said, "Are you going to school the first day, Sam?"

"No, sir. I'm done going to school. I don't like it."

"Why, I just loved to go to school and learn from Mary McLaughlin," said Rosanna. "I hope they have a good teacher here, for I want to be a teacher too someday."

Bishop Shem looked up in surprise but merely said, "So?" Rosanna did not like the upward inflection of his voice that seemed to mean, "We'll see about that." She knew that the Amish were not favorable to education beyond the eighth grade, but she had never talked to her new foster father about it. Nothing more was said at the table, but Elizabeth sensed trouble ahead. She knew how determined Rosanna was to become a teacher, and she also knew the bishop's awkward position. As the head of a church opposed to education, he could hardly allow a member of his own household to become a teacher.

That evening in the privacy of their room, Elizabeth told Shem about Rosanna's great desire to become a teacher. "I guess I am to blame," she admitted, "but you see she was really an orphan girl. I thought maybe someday she would have to make her own living and she could make it a little easier at teaching than in any other way. Besides, she learns very easy."

"I can't have anybody studying to be a schoolteacher in my house," said Shem, feeling the full responsibility of the church on his shoulders. How could he preach against "worldly wisdom" and allow a member of his own household to get all of it she could? It would put him in an embarrassing position and undermine his authority in the church. He could not permit that.

Elizabeth understood the situation. But how could she tell Rosanna! Next day Elizabeth sent Leah to the garden to weed the onions. She asked Rosanna to sit in the kitchen with her and sew rags together to make a rug. When they had worked quietly for a while, Elizabeth said, "Rosanna, I must tell you something that hurts me very much because I know it will hurt you, too. Shem asked me whether you really intend to become a schoolteacher. I told him what we had planned. He said that since the church is against worldly wisdom and education he could not allow anybody in his house to study to be a teacher. If he did, the people would blame him for not upholding the rules of the church. I can see, Rosanna, the position it puts him in. I guess you will have to give up being a teacher. I am so sorry, but I believe things will work out all right some other way. God never lets us suffer long if we trust His leadings."

"Oh, Momly, how can I ever give up being a teacher? I had my whole heart set on that work." Rosanna began to cry, but when she saw tears in Momly's eyes, she realized she was not bearing this disappointment alone. Her great love for Momly, her unlimited confidence in her, and the firm desire never to hurt her in any way, somehow gave Rosanna strength to dry her tears. All that the other family members ever knew of this great struggle was that the Irish lilt in Rosanna's laugh was missing for several days.

Shem sensed this. While he felt he had to be firm, he could still be sympathetic. For several days he tried to show Rosanna every consideration he could. He did one thing that proved to Rosanna that he was trying to be as nice to her as his position allowed. Every year traveling circuses came to Belleville. It was not against the rules of the church for Amish people to go to a circus if there were animals on exhibition. So Shem said to Elizabeth at the supper table, "There's a circus coming to town in a few days. There will be some tigers and lions and elephants and other animals to see. How would you like to take Leah and Rosanna to the circus to see the animals?"

Of course, it was understood that if you paid to see the animals, there was no reason, since you were right there anyway, why you should not go in and see the rest of the performance. But the argument was that God made the animals and surely it could not be wrong to go see them. About the rest of the show there was no argument, but nothing was said about it.

How Rosanna and Leah enjoyed the circus! They had never seen an elephant before and to see one swing his great trunk around and ward off flies amused them greatly. When they had looked at the tigers and the lions and the giraffe, they stood in front of the monkey cage a long time watching the monkeys leap from one perch to another and swing by their tails. Finally Leah said, *"Sie gooke schier wie Mänche"* (They look almost like people).

In the big tent they were hardly seated till a parade began led by the band. How that band music thrilled Rosanna! *"Wann ich danze keent, deht ich"* (If I could dance, I would).

Elizabeth was pleased to hear the ring in Rosanna's laugh again, for now she felt sure that Shem's gesture of peace was having its effect.

Rosanna was living down her greatest disappointment. While she was still heavy-hearted, she consoled herself with the thought of Cristal's comforting words, "All things work together for good to them that love the Lord."

At the supper table that evening Shem saw that his peace plan was working and he was inwardly relieved, for it hurt him to sadden Rosanna. As she told them about the animals and the band and the clowns, he could hear the familiar lilt in her laugh which he had missed so much during the last few days.

Rosanna learned to know a lot of girls her age at the preaching services. And what preaching services they had in Big Valley! Why, in summertime the houses were filled and sometimes they even had to put benches on the porch for some of the men. And the singing, what volume! Rosanna began to study German so she could sing, too. She loved music.

When preaching was at Reuben Kauffman's one Sunday, she was surprised to have Reuben come to her and say, "Why, Rosanna, how you have grown. I knew you when you were a little Irish baby. Baby Rosanna, we called you. I'm glad you came to Big Valley. Long ago your father asked me to look after you a little and I told him I would." Then he told her how he had moved to Big Valley from Half Moon Valley just about the time his Uncle Cristal and Elizabeth had moved to Lost Creek Valley.

Rosanna was delighted to have such a fine looking man come to her and tell her that he knew her when she was a baby in Half Moon Valley, and had known her father, Patrick McGonegal, and that he had taken her father and the three children to the railroad station at Bellefonte when they departed for Philadephia long ago. She had heard Reuben lead one of the hymns at preaching that day, and now she said to herself, "Just as soon as I can learn to read German I am going to ask Reuben to teach me the *Lob Sang.*" Because it is always used as the second hymn of every preaching service, young folks try to learn that hymn first. If they cannot

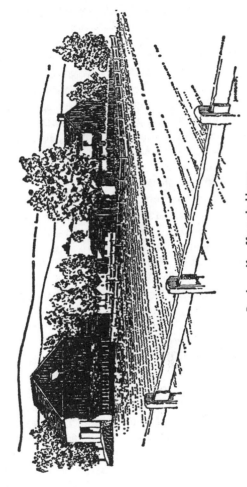

Reuben Kauffman's Home

learn to sing the *Lob Sang,* they might just as well give
up trying to learn any of the slow tunes, or hymns.

At preaching that day Rosanna learned to know two
sisters about her own age. They were Sarah and Franey
(Frances) Yoder, who lived just a field's breadth away,
at the big stone house. They were Lame Yost Yoder's
daughters. Rosanna heard these girls talking to some
others about beginning to join church in two weeks.
(Preaching was held in each congregation only every
two weeks.) She listened attentively, for she had promised Bishop Shem in Lost Creek Valley two years ago to
join church as soon as she was old enough. And maybe
she was old enough now.

When they had returned from preaching that Sunday
and Rosanna was alone with Momly she said, "Momly,
today at preaching I heard Lame Yost's girls, Sarah and
Franey, saying about twenty boys and girls will begin
joining church in two weeks. Do you think I would be
old enough to join now?"

Momly thought for a moment and then said, "I can
hardly believe you are sixteen years old already. How
quickly you have grown up. If you feel like joining
church now, I would be glad." And in two weeks Rosanna was one of those who began joining church. What
a joy it was to belong to a group of twenty young folks
who were bound together by a common purpose. She
liked the girls; they were all dressed alike. Each girl
wore a black cap, a white kerchief bound around the
waist and folded over the breast and brought up tight
around the neck, and a white apron. In these details
they were all alike but some had blue dresses, and others brown, dark red, or black. But no matter what the
color was, they were all perfectly plain with no figures
or flowers, and every dress cut after the same pattern.
The skirt was long and full, the body tight fitting, the
sleeves long and rather close fitting, and each dress had

a little tuck in the center of the back at the waist line called a *Läplei*. Each girl wore an apron almost as long as her skirt, fastened around the waist with a single apron string about an inch wide, and pinned at the side.

The boys wore a *Muhtze,* a sort of cutaway coat, and broad-fall pants. Their hair reached an inch below the ear lobe, and each boy had to begin letting his beard grow. Any young person unwilling to comply with these requirements would not be considered for membership.

Rosanna and the others were required to come to the next six or seven regular preaching services for definite religious instruction. They went into the house each Sunday before church services began and were seated on benches reserved for them. The fellows sat on the bench just back of the one reserved for the ministers, and the girls sat just back of the boys. When the first hymn was announced and all the men had removed their hats and the singing began, the ministers withdrew to an upstairs room prepared for them and the group joining church followed.

There for twenty minutes or a half hour the bishop instructed them on the plan of salvation, baptism, foot washing, communion, nonresistance, nonswearing, nonconformity, separation from the world, and the godly life in general.

After six or seven Sundays of instruction, each member of the group was asked whether he was willing to conform to the rules of the church and whether he still wished to become a member of the church. Those who answered "Yes," as they always do, were considered eligible for baptism on the following Sunday.

On the Sunday the young folks were to be taken into the church, preaching services were held at Lame Yost Yoder's home, just across the field from Rosanna's home. Bishop Shem and his family walked to preaching

Little Crist's Birthplace, or Lame Yost's House

that day. Lame Yost Yoder lived in the large stone house built by Captain John Armstrong on the two thousand acre tract received from the William Penn Estate for his services in the French and Indian War. This house was built about 1770 and was purchased from the Captain in 1796 by Joseph Yoder of Earl Township, Lancaster County, Pennsylvania. It has remained in the Joseph Yoder family for more than a century and a half.

When they arrived at preaching about half past eight on that special Sunday morning, the August sun was already hot. Rosanna opened her cap strings as she walked, hoping she might be a little cooler. The large barnyard was already almost filled with white and yellow top carriages. Yost had seen to it that his two boys, Christian and Eli, had everything in tiptop shape. The barnyard was raked and swept, the stables cleaned, the entries swept, the manure pile built up straight on every side, and all farm machinery strictly in its place.

As the boys were busy unhitching horses and taking them to the stables, Eli called out, "My golly, Crist, what will we do? The stables are almost full already and just look at that string of carriages coming in the lane!"

"When the stables are full, put the horses into the barn floor, and when that is full tie them to the barnyard fence and give them hay. That's the best we can do," said little Christian, oldest son of Lame Yost Yoder. By nine o'clock everything was full and many of the carriages had to be placed in the field adjoining the barnyard. Christian called to Eli, "You boys will have to take care of the horses now. I must go in. They are beginning to sing." Christian belonged to the group that was joining church, so he had to be there when the ministers withdrew to the upstairs room for instruction.

In a few minutes the great stone house was filled to overflowing and Reuben Kauffman announced the first hymn. All hats were removed and men's and women's voices singing in unison filled the house. The ministers rose and led the way to the upstairs room, followed by the twenty young folks who were to be baptized and taken into the church that day. Rosanna thought she had never heard such wonderful singing.

This was the last meeting with the ministers in private counsel and instruction. "Dress plainly according to the rules of the church," Bishop Shem reminded them. "Abstain from all worldly amusements—entertainments, festivals, ball games, and dances. Avoid profanity, vulgarity, boasting, and gossip. Abstain from drinking, and carousing, and, above all, yielding to the lust of the flesh. Let your conversation be mild and modest, your conduct kind and gentle, and all your actions dominated by the Golden Rule. Tell the truth. Your word must never be questioned. Walk soberly and let your light shine before the world so that they may see your good works and glorify your heavenly Father."

Every young man and young woman felt the weight of the bishop's words, and the solemn gravity of the step they were about to take. The young folks were given a final opportunity to express their willingness to obey the rules of the church. Then they were dismissed to go downstairs and take the places reserved for them, the two benches just back of the ministers' bench.

The order of services on this baptismal day were the same as usual. Christian L. Yoder preached first. This was followed by silent prayer.The Scripture was read by deacon John Hostetler, while the congregation stood. The main sermon was delivered by Bishop Shem, who spoke mostly on the duties of young people entering the Christian life, quoting freely from the Bible and the New Testament.

After he had preached a little over an hour Bishop Shem said, "Today we solemnize the rite of baptism.

Twenty young folks have expressed their faith in God, have promised to obey the rules of the church, have requested baptism, and have asked to be taken into the church. Let us pause a moment. If any member knows any good reason why any one of these applicants should not be received into the church, let him speak now, for after this no complaint will be heard." After a brief pause he said, "There seems to be no objection from any member. We will now prepare for baptism."

The deacon went out and returned with a pitcher of water. The applicants stood up, the benches were pushed aside, and they all kneeled in a line before Bishop Shem, who remained standing. When all was ready the bishop said, "Do you believe that Jesus Christ is the Son of God?" and each applicant replied in turn, "I believe that Jesus Christ is the Son of God."

"Do you promise by the help of God to renounce the world, the flesh and the devil, to obey the rules of the church, and live faithfully according to the Scriptures?" In turn again each one answered, "I do."

The bishop then stepped up to the first young man in line, and held his hands funnel-like above his head while the deacon poured water through the bishop's hands three times as the bishop said, "Daniel (using the first name only of the applicant), I baptize you in the name of the Father, and of the Son, and of the Holy Ghost." The deacon timed the three pourings to coincide with the mention of the three names of the Godhead. The bishop then took the young man by the hand and said, "In the name of the Father arise." Then he greeted the young man with the Holy Kiss and invoked God's blessing upon him. He repeated the same ceremony with each of the other young men.

In an Amish baptismal service, when the bishop comes to the young women, his wife comes forward, removes the young woman's cap, and the bishop places his hands above her head. The deacon pours water three times and the bishop says, "Mary, I baptize thee," etc., as before. The bishop's wife then replaces the young woman's cap, takes her by the right hand and says, "In the name of the Father arise." She then kisses the young woman and invokes God's blessing upon her. They repeat the ceremony with each young woman in turn.

When Bishop Shem had finished baptizing the young men, Elizabeth came forward to assist him with the girls. She did her part with grace and poise till she came to Rosanna. When she removed Rosanna's cap, her eyes filled with tears. Even Bishop Shem, who had baptized scores of young folks, could scarcely control his own voice and emotions as he said, "Rosanna, I baptize thee in the name of the Father, and of the Son, and of the Holy Ghost." As Elizabeth replaced Rosanna's cap and took her by the right hand saying, "In the name of the Father arise," her voice broke. As she kissed Rosanna she put her strong arm about Rosanna for just a moment and in a broken whisper said, "God bless you." As the people looked on, there was hardly a dry eye in the house. Some of the older women said softly through their tears, *"Wie die Lisbet doch des Medlie liebt"* (How dearly Elizabeth loves that little girl).

When the baptismal service was finished, the benches were put back in place, the young folks seated, and the sermon continued for some time. Then all kneeled while the bishop read the prayer from the prayer-book. After the prayer everyone stood up. The benediction was pronounced. Everyone bowed deeply bending the knee, and was seated. The deacon then announced the home where preaching would be held in two weeks. The closing hymn was sung and when the last sound had died away, the men arose slowly, put on their hats, and slowly moved out of the house and into the yard and out to the barn. The women adjourned to the porches and to the summer house to make room for those whose duty it was to set the table and serve the dinner. Preaching was "out" and twenty young members had been added to the congregation.

As the people finished their dinners, the white and yellow top carriages began to move out the lane in long rows. Bishop Shem stood in the houseyard talking to some of the older men. When he saw Elizabeth and the girls, Rosanna and Leah, coming through the yard, he joined them and they headed for home across the field.

As they walked through the outer barnyard, Rosanna could not help noticing Little Crist. He had resumed his duties—going for horses, hitching them up, and helping people get on their way. While he was not tall, he was well built, with light wavy hair, blue eyes, and red cheeks. Rosanna had noticed him before. But today as she saw him move about his work with such ease and enthusiasm, she thought to herself that he was about the nicest young man she had seen in the Kishacoquillas Valley. But what of it? It was not time yet for her to think about the boys.

In the evening when the benches (*Gemeh Benk*) had been put away and all the furniture put back in its place and the family sat in the living room tired, Sarah said, "Franey, didn't you think Rosanna McGonegal looked pretty nice today with her black wavy hair and red cheeks?"

"Yes, I think she's a beauty," said Franey.

"What did you think of her, Crist?"

"None of your business," said Little Crist blushing. The girls tittered as though they knew a secret.

"Don't mind the girls," said his mother. *"Sie sin glene Bapel Meiler"* (They are little blabbermouths). Christian said nothing more, but he knew what he was thinking.

CHAPTER 8

New Joys

AS the hot September days began to shorten and the evenings became longer, Momly said, "Girls, there's a saying that when the wind blows over the oats stubbles, the women must begin working in the evening. The oats stubbles have already been plowed under. Rosanna, you may do the patching and the darning, and, Leah, you may get your knitting. I want you to knit your father a pair of woolen stockings for Christmas. I will show you how to make the stitches." Rosanna had already learned to knit stockings; so as soon as her mending was finished, she began a pair of stockings for herself.

The autumn nights were becoming more chilly, and Rosanna knew that it would not be long now until the big frost. Chestnut burs would crack open; chestnuts would fall, and there surely would be some chestnut parties. Long rows of corn shocks waited in the field. Maybe Bishop Shem would pay her a little for each shock she husked and that would give her some money for Christmas and winter. Then, too, there might be some cornhuskings and maybe Momly would let her go to one.

Rosanna was thrilled with the thought of the good times just ahead. Soon she would ask Momly to let her and Leah go to a Sunday evening singing. She had never been to one yet, and how she did love to sing with a large group of people. At a singing she could talk to more people than at preaching. She could learn to know more of the young folks and to sing new tunes.

But Rosanna had one disappointment to live down. When the school bell rang in the morning it seemed to say, "Rosanna, come to school," and how she did want to go. But Momly said it would be wrong to go now that she had joined church. She certainly did not want to do anything that was wrong and certainly Momly knew what was best. And with that she began to sing and think of the singings and the cornhuskings that she know Momly would let her go to soon. It was a joyous world after all.

One day Rosanna received a letter from Philadelphia. It was from her brother William. Now that she understood Momly was not her real mother, she realized that William and John were her real brothers and that Margaret was her sister. As she grew older she began to feel a longing, a sort of secret tie, binding her to them. She wanted to see them all, knowing that they really belonged to each other. She would write to William—to all of them—and tell them what a happy home she had —nice clothes, so many good friends, joy in her religious life, and Momly, what a mother Momly was!

When the men had gotten the cornhusking well under way, Shem said at the dinner table one day, "Girls, if you will help husk corn, I will pay you two cents for each shock you husk, and we will 'tear down' and bind the fodder." They were delighted. Every day, just as soon as Momly could spare them, the girls went to the cornfield. Rosanna had nimble hands, and when the men prepared the shocks for her, she could husk twenty-five shocks per day. "Why," said Rosanna, "that's fifty cents per day. I'll soon have plenty to buy a new dress and new shoes, with money left over."

Shem knew that he would have to buy clothes for the girls anyway, and paying them for helping with the corn, gave them a feeling of independence and self-respect.

At the breakfast table one morning Sam said, "I was in town yesterday evening and young Crist Yoder told me there's going to be a cornhusking at Reuben Kauffman's on Thursday evening." The girls could hardly hide their excitement, but they did not want to appear too anxious.

When the morning work was done, the girls came to Momly before going to the cornfield and said, "Momly, may we go to the cornhusking at Reuben Kauffman's on Thursday evening?"

"Will you stay out of trouble?"

"Oh, yes, indeed we will."

"Jah, well," said Momly.

"Oh, good," laughed the girls. They couldn't contain their joy any longer. As they scampered out to the cornfield they plotted how they could persuade Sam to take them to the cornhusking. They agreed to ask him, "Will you take us to the cornhusking, *if* Momly lets us go?" He'll say "Yes" to that. He'll think Momly won't let us go, and he'll not need to take us. When they arrived in the cornfield Leah said, "Sam, if Momly lets us go, will you take us to the cornhusking Thursday evening?"

Sam replied, "Yes, *if* Momly lets you go." The girls giggled and Bishop Shem said to Sam, *"Now, hen sie dich"* (Now they've got you). Sam looked a little sheepish, but he couldn't back down now.

When Thursday evening came, the girls quickly washed the supper dishes, ran upstairs and put on their brown dresses, white caps, and black kerchiefs and aprons. For social occasions they reversed the colors of their caps and aprons. For church it was always black caps and white kerchiefs and aprons.

When they arrived at Reuben's a number of fellows and girls were already in the field. It was a beautiful October evening with a bright full moon. The boys "tore down" the shocks and then each one asked a girl to help him husk. In that way each boy chose his partner. If girls were not immediately chosen, they began to husk anyway. Soon a boy would come along and seeing an attractive girl not yet chosen he would say, "Need any help?" If the girl liked him, she would say, "Sure I do." If she didn't, she would say, "My helper is coming soon." That meant, "Pass on, buddy. I'm not interested."

Reuben Kauffman, being the man of the house, was out in the field directing the work somewhat. When he saw Rosanna and Leah coming into the field, he welcomed them and chatted pleasantly. He knew that this was Rosanna's first party, and he was anxious that she have a good time and get started right. "Do you have a partner, Rosanna?" he asked.

"No, we just arrived," she said.

"I know a fine partner for you. He just came and is not husking yet." Reuben felt a great interest in Rosanna, for he knew her when she was a baby in Half Moon Valley. He recalled Patrick McGonegal's parting words to him at the Bellefonte railroad station, "Reuben, ye'll be lookin' after baby Rosanna a bit too, won't you?" Reuben walked over to where some boys were standing and said, "Come here, Cristly." Christian Yoder came at once, and Reuben said, "Cristly, why don't you husk with Rosanna McGonegal?" Cristly was obviously pleased.

Cristly walked over to where the girls were standing and said to Rosanna, "I need a partner. Will you help me?"

"Yes," said Rosanna. "Could you get a partner for Leah?"

Cristly soon had a partner for Leah and they were off —Cristly and Rosanna at one shock and Leah and her partner at another. Cristly soon saw that Rosanna knew how to husk corn. Between talking about Lost Creek Valley, and the different members of the group who had joined church with them, and racing to finish first, they had a wonderful time. There were many young folks at the husking and there was much laughing everywhere, for whenever a red ear of corn was found the boy had to kiss his partner. Cristly wished he could find a red ear in his shock but, unfortunately, none appeared. He would gladly have done his duty, for to him Rosanna with her bright eyes and red cheeks was a beautiful girl.

While the young people were husking corn, Lydia, Reuben's wife, and a number of helpers were preparing supper. About ten o'clock she sent word out to Reuben that supper was ready and Reuben called out, "Everybody in for supper." A cheer of joy went up as they hurried to finish their shock of corn. As they finished, each boy escorted his partner to the table. Tables were set up in every available space so that the entire group could be seated at once. When all were seated, Reuben said, "Let us return thanks," and every head was bowed in silent grace.

For supper Lydia served great platters of stewed beef with plenty of gravy, mashed potatoes, sweet potatoes, fried mush, beet pickles, large slices of bread from big oven-baked loaves, and for dessert large pieces of fresh grape pie.

Reuben had swept the barn floor and had hung lanterns from the "overden," for he knew that as soon as supper was over, the young folks would want to go to the barn and play party games—Bingo, Six-Handed Reel, O-Hi-O, Twin Sisters, Skip to Ma Lou, and maybe a little old-fashioned Ring. Some of the boys had not found red ears of corn and here would be a chance to make up for the loss. Rosanna had never heard these party songs. She was especially delighted with the rhythm of O-Hi-O. Cristly was her partner for the first play, but soon other boys came around. When they played Six Handed Reel, Ben Sharp was her partner. Ben was tall and husky and when they "balanced off" she thought Ben would swing her off her feet. What a wonderful evening—songs she had never heard, action she had never seen, and new friends that showed her every consideration.

When the clock pointed to 1:30 a.m., Sam came around and said, "Get ready, girls. It's time to go home." When Rosanna and Leah got to their room, it was a little after two o'clock. Tired? Yes, but happy. Rosanna had resolved to have nothing to do with the boys until after she was seventeen. But as she dozed off, the thought that the nicest boy at the party, the one everybody called Little Crist, had been her partner, was pleasing to her.

In the cornfield the next day the girls were pretty sleepy, but they tried hard to keep up their usual pace. If a party unfitted them for work, they knew Momly would not be inclined to let them go next time. One could afford to make almost any kind of sacrifice for pleasure like that. For that reason they used every ounce of will power to keep awake and to keep going. Evening seemed a long time in coming. When the supper dishes were done, two sleepy girls asked whether they might not put off the knitting till tomorrow evening. Momly smiled. *"Jah, well,"* she agreed.

Rosanna and Leah had never been to a Sunday evening singing. As they heard others talk of them, they had a great desire to go to one, but would they dare ask permission so soon after the cornhusking? Leah had an idea. "Rosanna, I think I heard pap say that preaching will be at our house in three weeks. Let's get the boys to ask him to have a singing here in the evening. They generally have a singing in the evening at the same place where preaching was held that day. Then we'll *be* at the singing and we'll not need to ask Momly to go." Rosanna thought it was a fine idea. They told Sam about it, and he agreed to help.

Preparing for preaching was soon uppermost in the family mind, and it was a strenuous job. The houseyard was raked and swept; every porch was scrubbed with silver sand to make it white and immaculate. On Wednesday a few women came to help scour the tinware. On Friday others came to help bake great loaves of bread in the big oven. On Saturday a dozen women came to help bake apple pies and half-moon pies. All day Saturday the menfolks were busy cleaning the stables and the barnyard and getting the "preaching benches" down and dusting them thoroughly. Early on Sunday morning the men removed all partitions, placed the benches all through the house, and put the big German hymnbooks, *The Ausbund*, on the singers' table. It was a busy week.

Sam was responsible for placing the carriages and unhitching the horses. He had asked Ben Sharp and Siever Yoder to help him. This gave him a chance to say to these boys, "The girls would like to have a singing here this evening. Will you boys ask pap?" The boys were eager to cooperate. When preaching was "out" and dinner was being served, the boys watched for Bishop Shem. As he came out from the first table, the boys approached him and said, "Shem, we would like to have a singing here this evening. Are you agreed?"

He did not dare seem too easily convinced, so he answered, "Ach, what do you want a singing for?"

"We want to learn some new tunes, and your son Yost knows so many tunes, and we thought maybe he would be willing to stay, bein's the singin' is here, and learn us some."

"*Jah, well,*" said Shem. He liked his son Yost. He was one of the acknowledged leaders of singing and the boys knew this mention of Yost was good strategy. Yost was already married, and married folks did not usually attend singings, but when Yost was appealed to from the angle of teaching some new tunes, he could not resist. He was willing to sit and sing by the hour on almost any occasion, but especially when someone wanted to learn from him.

Soon after the early autumn sunset, the buggies began coming in over the hill. The boys were bringing their sisters and maybe a sister's friend, but not their own girl friends. Boys are rarely if ever seen driving in daytime with their own girl friends. The greatest possible secrecy surrounds their social relations. The one time when hedging on telling the truth is permissible is when a boy is charged with having a "girl" or when a girl is charged with having a beau. Both will deny the accusation to the last even though they know it is true. That is why they never want to be together alone in daytime. They do not take their "girls" to singing, but they do take them home afterwards. A boy never goes to his girl's home in daytime alone, and he does not enter the house in the evening when he calls on her till after her parents have retired.

At a singing two or three tables are set end to end along one side of the living room for the singers. The girls sit back of the table along the wall while the boys sit on the other side. Even though only German hymns are sung, a singing is not a religious service, but during the singing of any hymn all persons present are supposed to join in the singing or abstain from conversation. Sometimes the boys forget and annoy the singers by talking too loudly making it necessary for the man of the house to say, "Let us have order."

As Rosanna and Leah were hostesses this evening, they did not sit at the singers' table but left the room for visiting girls. Yost Yoder, the singer, took his place at the head of the table. Next to him was Little Crist and Ben Sharp and other young men who were anxious to learn to sing. Back of the table were the girls. Hannah Yoder, the singer's daughter, had a wonderful voice, clear and resonant. Beside her were Sarah and Franey, Little Crist's sisters, and many others, filling the table entirely. When the tables were filled, as others came they stood back of the young men, both boys and girls, until there were nearly a hundred voices singing.

Yost's first selection was, *Weil nun die Zeit vorhanden ist* (While Now the Time Is at Hand). It was one of the easy slow tunes and appears on the next page.

These slow tunes are very difficult to sing. They are a holdover from the Alsatian Chorale or the Pyrinnean Chorale, or the Gregorian Chants which originated in Germany in the early part of the seventeenth century. When the Amish people left Alsace-Lorraine because of religious persecution late in the seventeenth century, they brought these chorales along to America and have used them unchanged ever since. There is no part singing. Everyone sings in unison. Since the Amish do not have these chorales set to music, they must be passed on from generation to generation by memory. Consequently only boys and girls with a keen sense of pitch and sound can ever learn to sing them and many can never learn them well enough to "lead" in singing.

Little Crist and Ben Sharp wanted to learn to lead so they followed with great care. After two stanzas had been sung, Yost turned to Little Crist and said, "Now, Cristly, you lead the next verse and if you 'stall,' I'll help you out." Cristly took the same pitch and led off.

Weil nun die Zeit vorhanden ist.

Song: "Weil nun lie Zeit vorhanden ist"

He got along fine for the first three lines but when he
swung into the fourth line, he ran into trouble. But
Yost's strong voice picked up the tune instantly, put
Cristly back on the tune. He finished all right but was
rather flustered. Next Ben Sharp with still less experience wanted to try the *Lob Sang,* always sung as the
second hymn at preaching service. Since this hymn must
be sung every Sunday, it is more familiar than others.
That's why beginners try leading it as their first attempt.
Ben started out with colors flying, but before he was
through Yost had to help him get through it too. The
Lob Sang appears on page 98.

After they had sung several of the slow chorales, one
of the girls announced, *Wo Ist Jesus mein Verlangen,* to
the tune of, "What a Friend We Have in Jesus." The
"fast" tunes are easily sung, but the chorales must be
learned for preaching services; no fast tunes are ever
sung there. Siever Yoder announced, *Jesu, Jesu, Brun
des Lebens,* to the tune of, "Come Thou Fount of Every
Blessing." Everybody knew these familiar words and
the tune and joined in heartily. Even those in the kitch-
en and on the porches sang until the house seemed to
vibrate with melody. Rosanna was thrilled almost to
tears! She knew some German and joined in the singing
joyously.

Between hymns or chorales pleasant conversation is
always permissible; it is an informal meeting. When ten
o'clock came, Yost arose to leave the table. That was a
signal for the others and in a few minutes everybody
was visiting merrily or getting ready to go home. The
girls gathered near the door and presently one boy after
another walked up to his "girl," extended his arm and
out they went together. Boys brought their own sisters
to singing but other boys took them home. Thus the
singing affords not only an opportunity to learn the
hymns of the church, but a pleasant time socially where

boys and girls get acquainted, make friends, choose companions, and eventually get married.

Bishop Shem and Momly sat near the bedroom door enjoying the singing. The bishop spoke pleasantly to the young people as they approached him. They respected him both as their spiritual leader and their friend. But Momly had the double pleasure of hearing the singing and seeing Rosanna so filled with happiness that she could hardly contain herself. A little mist dimmed her eyes as she thought of Rosanna, the little Irish Catholic baby; her father going off to find a place for the other children; his accidental death so that he never came for the baby; the other children in Philadelphia, now grown to manhood and womanhood, faithful members of the Catholic Church; and Rosanna, so different! Had she done right to bring her up Amish? But what else could she do? She had followed God's leading from day to day, and this is where it brought her. She believed it was pleasing in His sight; she was content.

When the young folks had all departed, Rosanna slipped over and sat on the arm of Momly's rocking chair. Putting her arm around Momly's shoulder she said, *"Hav Ich mich recht ag'shickt"* (Did I behave right?).

"Jah, Ich bin zufride" (I'm satisfied). Rosanna kissed Momly on the cheek and ran upstairs to join Leah. Rosanna said to Leah, "My! Isn't it nice just to be alive. Isn't it wonderful to sing like we sang tonight! Why sometimes I felt as if my body was getting so light I couldn't keep my feet on the floor. I thought sometimes the singing would just carry me away! Singing, friends, church, home! Isn't life beautiful!"

Next day Bishop Shem had business at the blacksmith shop. When he entered, Jesse Horton, the rugged blacksmith, a deacon in the Lutheran Church, said,

Der Lobgesang.

Song: "Der Lobgesang"

"Bishop, I want to thank you for the beautiful singing you furnished us last night."

"Could you hear it down here?" asked the bishop, astounded.

"Yes, sir! The sound of the singing came rolling down along the creek like a great, heavenly anthem. It lifted my soul to the very gates of heaven and I could not help but say, 'Hallelujah.' My, it was wonderful. Don't we Christians have joys that the world knows nothing about? I couldn't understand the German words, but I caught the spirit of the singing. I don't believe, Bishop, that any secular singing can ever have such spiritual fervor and such moral uplift as the singing of those young people last night had."

The bishop smiled with satisfaction.

"And how well behaved your young folks are!" the blacksmith continued. "After the singing was over, dozens of buggies drove out the road past my house and I never heard a loud word out of any one of those young people. Bishop, I rejoice that you Amish people are able to train your young folks so well."

CHAPTER 9

Young Womanhood

AS Rosanna thought of these new joys and friends, and her relation to the church now that she had been baptized, she began to have the feeling of being grown up. Already her reputation as a good worker was widely known so that when people found themselves in great need of household help, they would ask her to help them.

While it was a means of earning extra money, yet

Momly did not feel that she wanted Rosanna to be considered as a maid for anybody and everybody to hire. She made it a rule to let Rosanna go only when there was an emergency and then only for a week or two at the most. In that way Momly felt that she could cultivate in her a finer feeling of self-respect and make her a happier woman. She knew, of course, that girls serving as housemaids were not looked down on in any way among the Amish, but were on the same level socially as the rest of the family. It was even considered a mark of fine accomplishment to be able to step into a home and do any kind of work rapidly and well.

As Momly thought about it she reasoned, "We have always been together, and now that I am getting older and need her more at home, why should I let her work for other people all the time? Besides, the way things look, I suppose she will get married someday and then I will have to give her up."

Rosanna, for her part, had a keen sense of obligation to Momly. All that Rosanna was and all that she ever hoped to be was due entirely to Momly's noble example and loving guidance.

As the autumn leaves were turning from green to gold and scarlet and somber brown, preaching services were to be held at Nicholas Yoder's along the front Jack's Mountain. It was the time for fall communion. Rosanna and Leah had been looking forward to their first communion. After they participated in communion, they would be considered full members of the church, having partaken of all its ordinances.

At the supper table on Saturday evening Bishop Shem said, "Tomorrow is Communion Sunday. We will have to start to preaching a little early. Let's get everything ready this evening so we can start by half past seven in the morning."

When half past seven arrived Sunday morning, the

womenfolks were all dressed and ready. Sam had the big bay horse hitched to the white top carriage for his father and Momly while he and the girls followed in his buggy.

As they were crossing the low plateau running lengthwise through the valley, they could see across the long hollow to the home of Nicholas Yoder. White and yellow top carriages and open buggies were gathering from all directions—the Kauffmans and the Zooks from down the valley, the Peacheys and the Hartzlers from up the valley, the Yoders and the Bylers from the Stone Mountain, the Detweilers and the Kanagys from the front Jack's Mountain, to say nothing of the Riehls, the Swareys, the Rennos, and the Hostetlers from all parts of the valley.

By half past eight Bishop Shem and the ministers began to move toward the house, followed by the old men. Other groups followed and in a few minutes the services began. The familiar strains of the singing could be plainly heard at the barn, and it served as a plain hint to all the young men and boys still there that it was time to go to the house.

The order of services on communion day is slightly different from regular preaching services in that it requires three ministers instead of two. The first one opens the meeting. This is followed with the silent prayer. The second one quotes and comments on long passages from the Bible which relate to the children of Israel searching for the Promised Land. The third minister, usually the bishop, dwells on the sufferings of Christ and explains communion, the bread and wine, and the practice of foot washing. The last two sermons are mental and physical strains since so much of the Scripture must be quoted verbatim. Some ministers work so hard at their preaching that their clothing becomes saturated with perspiration as they preach.

The preaching is continuous, but when the noon hour arrives, a table is set in the summer house and one by one both men and women go out, get a bite to eat—bread, hot coffee, pies, beets, and pickles—and then return to their places.

Since Christ was crucified about three o'clock in the afternoon, the Bishop tries to terminate his sermon about that time and serve communion. When that time approaches, the deacon goes out and brings in the bread and the wine. After the bread has been blessed by prayer, the bishop and some of the ministers pass the bread to each member. After the bread has been served, the wine is blessed in the same way, and in the same manner is passed to each member till all are served. While the bread and wine are being passed, the bishop usually repeats some Scripture pertaining to the communion in low voice as though encouraging the members in good works. When the bread and wine have been passed, the services are closed in much the usual way—testimony from all ministers and deacons present, a few closing words from the bishop, prayer, and the closing hymn.

The closing communion hymn always is *Vo'm Hertzen will Ich Singen* (From the heart will I sing). Just before this hymn is announced, the deacon goes out and brings in towels and two pails containing warm water. While this hymn is being sung the men pair off and wash each other's feet in the room where the ministers sit. When each has washed the other's feet, they extend the right hand of fellowship and salute each other with the holy kiss. The one says, "God be with us," and the other answers, "Amen. Peace be with us." When they have put on their shoes, they go to a receptacle provided for alms and leave an offering for the support of the poor if there are any.

While the deacon brings in pails of water for the

men, the hostess provides pails and towels in the kitchen for the women. There the women observe the ordinance of foot washing in the same manner as the men do in the other room. When the different members have observed the foot washing ordinance and have given their offering, they are at liberty to leave the services. When the last couple has finished, the hymn is closed and services are over, usually about half past four or five o'clock in the afternoon.

Rosanna was so impressed with her first communion that when it came time to go home she came to Momly and said, *"Ich will mit dir Hehm geh"* (I want to go home with you). When her emotions were stirred, nothing soothed her so much as just to be with Momly. She had listened attentively as Bishop Shem explained that the bread stood for the broken body of Christ, the wine for His shed blood, and the foot washing for a life of humble service, and she was deeply moved. As they drove back home the big bay held his proud head high. He was all life and eager to go. But in the carriage Momly and Shem and Rosanna were still held by the solemn spell of the communion service, and they were silent.

As the Christmas season approached, Rosanna noticed strange young men and women at church and at singings. She was told that they were "Peckwayers," young Amish folks from that part of Lancaster County drained by the Pequea Creek. They were usually young folks who had come to the valley to visit. If they did not have any relatives, they came with someone who did, and they visited their relatives with them.

Since Lancaster County has so many Amish, one group frequently did not know that other groups were visiting. Sometimes three or four groups were in the valley at once and that made a good many visitors. But at this time of year the valley folks were well provided with fresh meats from the fall butcherings, canned fruits and dried corn and tomatoes, large bins of potatoes and apples. The food problem, outside of the preparation, was not a serious one.

These young folks dressed just like the valley young folks except that the girls pinned their kerchiefs straight down over the breast instead of folding them over, and the boys wore their hair a little shorter and trimmed their beards a little closer. Sometimes the ministers and the bishop in the valley looked somewhat askance at these young folks, fearing that they might have a little pride in their neatness and might sow some of that seed in the minds of the valley young people. Most of them were fine singers. The boys played corner ball very well, but the valley boys could surpass them in wrestling.

Rosanna and Leah heard that there was going to be a corner ball game at Christian Sharp's, the home of tall, husky Ben Sharp, on Thursday afternoon. The Pequea boys were going to play the valley boys and after the game there might be some friendly wrestling. Since Sam was going anyway, Momly agreed that the girls might just as well go too. Rosanna and Leah were delighted.

It was a sunny afternoon in January. Ben had just covered the broad manure pile with fresh clean straw, and everything was ideal for a good game. The valley boys drew corners first and as they passed the ball around swiftly and then threw it at one of the two Pequea boys in the "middle" they were surprised to see how these Pequea boys could dodge the ball. Ben Stultzfus was probably the best at dodging the ball. When the ball was thrown low at him he would jump into the air, almost turn a somersault, clearing the ball by two or three feet. When the ball was thrown high he would drop so quickly that the ball would shoot over him and miss again. When the valley boys had exhaust-

ed their corner force, they had to take their turns in the
"middle." Again they were surprised to see how those
Pequea boys could throw a ball. They could look one
way and throw the ball the other with great accuracy,
hitting an opposing player with the ball without apparently looking at him. At first the game was rather
one-sided, but the valley boys were quick to learn and
by the time the game was ended the score was only
twenty-five to thirty in favor of the Pequea boys.

When the wrestling began, the tables were turned.
They threw their hats into a ring and the hats that
touched meant that the owners should wrestle. The first
bout came between Siever Yoder and the agile Ben
Stultzfus. Siever was not regarded as a good wrestler
and Ben was able to put him away rather easily. The
next match came between big Ben Sharp and John
Lantz, a big man, too. This looked interesting from the
beginning, but Ben knew the technique of "side-holt"
wrestling and it was not long till John Lantz went over
Ben Sharp's hip with a bang, and he was down.

The next match looked funny. John Fisher, a six-
footer, was to wrestle Little Crist Yoder. Fisher looked
at Little Crist with a bit of scorn in his eyes. The Pequea boys grinned but the valley boys winked at each
other with perfect confidence. When they were ready,
Fisher swung Little Crist as if to throw him away, but
Crist leaped across his outstretched foot with ease,
landing on his feet in perfect position to counter with a
backward trip which laid Fisher neatly on his back. A
shout went up from the valley young men and girls, for
the girls were all grouped under the "overshot" watching the game and the wrestling.

"Der gleh Deihenger" (The little scoundrel), said a
Pequea boy. "Throw me that way if you dare."

"Come on," said Little Crist. "I'm willing to try."

John Mast came forward with a confident swing. They took holds and Little Crist said, "Are you ready?"

"Go ahead," said Mast. With one quick twist Little Crist seemed to brace himself under Mast, lift him off his feet, swing him over his hip and Mast was down. Then both groups cheered, for Mast was the confident challenger.

Rosanna had been standing among the girls. When she saw Little Crist wrestle with boys so much larger than he was she almost held her breath, but when he downed the big fellows she could hardly conceal her delight. When one of the girls said to her, "I guess those Pequea boys don't know that Little Crist is one of the best wrestlers in the valley," she tried to answer indifferently, but the little Irish lilt in her laugh gave her away. It was a great afternoon. The Pequea boys won in corner ball and the valley boys won in wrestling. But whether they won or whether they lost mattered little, for they were playing for fun and laughter more than for victory.

One reason why Little Crist wanted to do his best in wrestling was because he had seen Rosanna at the game and talked to her for just a moment. He thought he never saw her look so beautiful. He noticed too that some of the Pequea boys were engaging her in conversation, especially that John Mast who had challenged him to wrestle. He felt especially glad now that he had downed Mast, for he thought it might have impressed Rosanna. When the wrestling was over, Rosanna confirmed his hopes. "I'm glad you threw Mast," she said. "I don't like him anyway." That declaration was a source of real pleasure to Little Crist. Putting all these things together he decided that he might not be an unwelcome caller to Rosanna on Saturday evening. The more he thought of it the more he decided that "there was everything to gain and nothing to lose." As Crist went home that evening he could not forget Rosanna's red cheeks, her bright eyes, and her winning smile. When Saturday evening came, he put on his best clothes and acted as indifferently and unconcerned as possible. He did not want to attract any attention, but his sister Sarah said, "Crist, I believe you're going down to see Rosanna tonight."

"No, I'm not. I'm just going to town a little while," he said, trying to convince her otherwise. But he could not quite hide the combined joy and guilt that played about his mouth. Sarah just looked wise and said, "Uh-ha."

When he got to Belleville, he saw some boys who teased him a bit too, but with a great effort at self-control he avoided suspicion. To throw them still further off the track after a little while he said, "Well, I believe I'll go home," and off he started for home. When he came in so early, Sarah and Franey looked surprised and he simply said, "I told you so." He yawned and headed upstairs apparently to go to bed. However, before coming into the house he had placed a ladder against his bedroom window. Instead of going to bed, he went down the ladder and through the fields to Shem Yoder's. He had put a few grains of corn in his pocket, and when he reached the house he made sure that the parents were in bed. Then he went to Rosanna's bedroom window, tossed a few grains of corn against the panes, and waited. In a moment he heard the window raised quietly. Rosanna whispered, "Who's there?"

He whispered back, "Crist Yoder."

"I'll be down in a minute," she said, trembling with excitement. In a few minutes the front door opened ever so softly and Little Crist tiptoed into the kitchen. Rosanna had felt all day that Little Crist might call that evening. She had made up her mind that if he did, she would be ready and she would invite him in. They sat in the kitchen by a very dim tallow candlelight, because the kitchen was farthest away from the bedroom where the old folks slept. They must not know. Secrecy was of utmost importance.

After they had sat a while and the kitchen grew a little chilly, Rosanna stirred the fire and put more wood into the stove. Little Crist said, "What's the use of putting wood into the stove? Aren't we going upstairs?"

"No," said Rosanna very gently, "we will do our visiting here."

Then Rosanna went on to say that Momly had talked to her about "bundling," the old custom of young folks going to bed together to keep warm when houses were poorly heated, but since houses are better built there is no need of keeping up a practice which is open to so much criticism. Momly said the practice among the Amish people was to go to bed fully clad, and while there was no known immorality the Amish preachers and parents wanted this custom abolished as it might lead to wrong and unhappiness.

"Momly says that Bishop Shem is very much opposed to bundling," Rosanna explained. "I would not disobey him for the world. Momly says that only a few of our people court that way anymore and she thinks that in a few years with the preachers preaching against it, and the parents talking against it, it will be entirely discontinued among our people."

Little Crist could see the reasonableness of Momly's teaching and he said thoughtfully, "I think you and Momly are right." The subject was never mentioned again.

They had a happy evening together talking about the cornhusking, the singings, the corner ball game, and especially the wrestling. Rosanna expressed surprise that Little Crist could throw a fellow as big as John Fisher, but he merely laughed and said, "The bigger they are, the harder they fall." He added that being short had some advantages too. The big fellows could hardly get a good hold on him, while he could get under them and throw them.

Rosanna asked what progress he was making with his singing. "I was up at Reuben Kauffman's a couple times lately," he replied, "and I think I know three of the slow tunes now so that I can lead them in preaching before long." While Crist was deeply interested in singing, his real interest was horses. He told Rosanna how he was studying horses, and that his father had an interesting horse doctor book. From it one could learn the age of a horse by his teeth, the type of horse that made the best buggy horse, the best horses for road and farm, where to look for the principal weaknesses and blemishes and everything about a horse worth knowing.

"When I get that book mastered, they can't fool me on horses," Little Crist declared. The conversation about the horse doctor book reminded Rosanna how she had once studied too, to become a teacher. When she told Crist about it, he complimented her by saying, "Well, I believe you would have been a fine teacher."

One o'clock came all too soon, which was plenty late for the first call. As he said good-night he added, "May I come again sometime?" Rosanna replied, "Maybe, if you want to."

As Little Crist walked home across the fields he experienced a feeling he had never known before. Wonderful joy and gladness and inspiration were surging through his whole soul and body. Every muscle was charged with super strength. He ran as lightly as a deer for pure joy. Rosanna's last words, "Maybe, if you want to," lingered like music in his heart and almost seemed to lift him from the ground as he ran.

When he reached home, everybody was sound asleep. He took off his shoes on the porch, opened the great

hall door slowly, tiptoed upstairs, and went to bed con-
gratulating himself that he had fooled his sisters, he had
made a good impression on Rosanna, and he had come
in without anybody knowing it.

Next morning at the breakfast table Little Crist put
on his most innocent look, but Eli and the girls seemed
to share a secret that annoyed him just a bit. When Eli
finally made some slight reference to a ladder, he was
suddenly aware that he had forgotten to remove the ladder from his window when he made his silent departure
in the evening. He blushed with embarrassment when
his mother said smiling, "People who play tricks must
have good memories."

CHAPTER 10

The Visit

AUTUMN soon cooled into winter. The leaves of gold
and brown could hold on no longer, and the trees in the
valley and on the mountain sides were bare. But another beauty was soon to come; in fact it had already arrived. As the wind whistled around the corner of the
barn it carried with it flakes of snow and it was not long
till the whole valley was wrapped in a mantle of white.

Just before Christmas, the trees were so covered with
a clinging snow that their branches looked as though
they had been carved out of white marble. The fence
posts looked like white fairies standing hand in hand
around the fields. When the morning sun shone on this
vast expanse of white with all its variations, the great
Kishacoquillas Valley surrounded by high snow-covered
mountains, looked like a real wonderland.

Sam had already prepared the big sled and on Sunday they would all go to preaching in it. He had filled the sled with clean straw. What fun it was to sit down in the sled, cover up with warm blankets, bed quilts, and well-tanned sheepskins and glide noiselessly along the road or through the fields behind two spirited horses. Nobody wanted to miss preaching when the snowy roads were well packed, and the horses delighted in showing their strength and speed. This was the time too 'or more singings and parties and for weddings. While Rosanna had enjoyed summer, she found winter still more enticing.

Little Crist's calls became more frequent. In fact, they became regular. Every two weeks on Saturday evening he went to see Rosanna. He still announced his arrival with a few grains of corn thrown against her bedroom window. No matter how long a young Amishman calls on a young woman, the tension of secrecy is never relaxed.

How he wished he could bring his beautiful black buggy horse hitched to his new sleigh and take Rosanna for a drive on Sunday afternoon, but it just was not customary to do it that way and custom had to be observed and maintained. But after singings and parties he would take her home, and how she loved to sit in his comfortable sleigh behind that glossy black horse, which took them so quietly, yet with considerable speed. (Quietly because sleigh bells are considered worldly and not allowed by the church.)

Rosanna hated to see the snow slowly disappear in the spring, but the green fields and the flowers and the warm sunshine seemed so beautiful to her too that the winter joys soon faded from her mind.

One day Rosanna walked to Belleville to do some shopping. She stopped at the post office and was delighted to have a letter from Philadelphia. It was from her brother William. As she read it, she was filled with excitement. William said he would come up to see her and Momly a few days in the summer at a time when it suited best to have him. Rosanna hurried home to tell Momly the good news. Momly, too, was glad that he was coming because she did not want Rosanna to be entirely separated from her family.

When they discussed the best time for his visit, the question was not when it would suit them best but what time in the summer would he get the most enjoyment out of his visit. They finally decided that the harvesttime would be most interesting, for then the cherries would be ripe, the early harvest apples would be ready to eat, the clover fields would be red with bloom and the wheat fields would be aglow with ripening grain. Besides, there would be ten or twelve harvest hands to cook for and one more at the table would hardly be noticed. William might enjoy talking to these hard working men, too. Rosanna wrote him at once and suggested that he come about the tenth of June and stay at least ten days. She wanted him to see Amish country life when it was most interesting.

Before heading for the Kishacoquillas Valley, William went to see his brother John and his sister Margaret to tell them about his journey. They were tremendously interested. John said, "Find out all you can about that hexing business and the signs they paint on their barns to keep the hexes away." Margaret wanted to know whether the Amish really paint the front farm gate blue when there is a marriageable daughter in the family, and whether they actually powwow to stop the flow of blood or to take away pain.

As William traveled by train from Philadelphia he recognized many things he had seen some ten or twelve years before on his first trip to Thompsontown and Jericho to see Rosanna when she was just nine years old.

Soon after passing Thompsontown, he found the train plunging into Jack's Narrows, the long waterway cut through the mountains by the Juniata River.

He was awed by the scene as he rode on the stage-coach from Reedsville to Belleville—the deep green cornfields, the silver green oats fields, just out in head, the rose red clover fields like great gardens, and the golden wheat fields waving majestically. He had never seen such splendor of color in nature nor had he ever known the scent of new-mown hay. He was deeply impressed by all he saw—the Susquehanna and the Blue Juniata, the towering mountains hemming in the winding Jack's Narrows, and now the broad expanse of the fertile, colorful Kishacoquillas.

As William walked across the hill from Belleville to Bishop Shem Yoder's house, he paused many times to enjoy the beauty of the landscape, so quiet, so clean, so peaceful! "Rosanna is better here than in the noisy city. I am glad Elizabeth did not let me take her back to Philadelphia with me when I visited her before," he mused.

Rosanna was watching for him, and when she saw a stranger coming in across the hill, she ran to meet him, so glad to see her real brother again. William took off his hat, put his arm around her, kissed her. "Rosanna, is it really you? How you've grown!" he exclaimed.

"Yes, William, I'm your sister."

As he looked at her more closely he said, "I'm sure you are. Nobody but the Irish could have hair and eyes and cheeks and a lilt like that. I have always prayed that the Virgin Mary would take care of you, and now I know she has."

"Maybe she has," said Rosanna, not well versed in the work of the Virgin Mary, "but I think Momly helped her a great deal."

"That's true. God bless her," William agreed, making the sign of the cross in front of his face. Rosanna did not know what that meant. She did not ask, but she was confident it was all right.

When they reached the house, Momly greeted William more cordially than was her custom. She was a woman of few words but she wanted William to know that he was most welcome. While she never could give Rosanna up, she did want Rosanna to keep in touch with her brothers and sister.

When the men came in to supper, Bishop Shem greeted William warmly and said, "William, I am glad you came to see Rosanna and us; you are very welcome." Sam came in and shook William's hand. In Sam's strong grip, William's white slender hand seemed lost.

William remembered that the titles "Mr." and "Mrs." are not used much among the Amish, so he called everybody by their first names, to the delight and satisfaction of Bishop Shem. When they sat down to the table, all bowed their heads in silent grace. William crossed his hands and seemed to feel the presence of God. When grace was finished, Bishop Shem said, "Now, William, reach and help yourself."

The supper was a marvel to William—large platters of fried ham (and such ham!), large platters of fried eggs, large pieces of homemade bread fresh from the oven, dishes of mashed potatoes, pitchers of gravy, stewed tomatoes and corn, and to top it all off, big pieces of new cherry pie and gingerbread. When the different ones were through eating, William noticed they did not leave the table. But when the last one had finished, they all bowed their heads again and he knew that it was the grace of thanksgiving.

William stayed for a week. As he watched Rosanna at work, he marveled at how much she did and how little it seemed to tire her. She milked the cows, worked in the garden, carried large buckets of milk to the pigs, fed the chickens and gathered the eggs, washed, ironed, baked, and even helped in the harvest field sometimes. When he asked Rosanna whether she ever got tired, she laughed and said, "Oh, a little, sometimes. But I do this kind of work all the time. I'm used to it and don't mind it."

William watched everything with great interest—six men mowing grass in a large field, turning hay and heaping it, pitching hay, and the harpoon hayfork taking up great loads of hay and dumping it into the mow.

Then wheat cutting came with four or five cradlers, six or eight men binding the sheaves, and two boys gathering sheaves while two men shocked the wheat. Twelve or fourteen men sat down to the table at once, but busy as they were, William noticed the silent grace was never omitted. He marveled at how fast and how much these men ate. When grace was finished, Bishop Shem would always say, "Now men, reach and help yourselves," and many of the men followed the suggestion literally.

During the noon hour after the meal sometimes two of these young huskies would tussel and the roughness with which they threw each other about made William respect their strength. These young Amish fellows were just as anxious to have William tell them about Philadelphia as he was anxious to know about the country. As he talked about the city at various times one or another of them would say, "My! I wish I could live in Philadelphy."

William noticed too that the harvest hands were not all Amish. The Amishmen all wore homemade clothes —white muslin shirts, broadfall pants, no suspenders, hooks and eyes on their coats and vests, high crowned, broadbrimmed homemade straw hats, long hair, and beards. If a man had short hair, William knew he was not Amish. Both groups worked well together. It was

generally conceded that because of their heavy work the
Amish were a little stronger and had a little more endurance than the others.

They told William about the time Isaac Axe, a tall
slender carpenter of the Lutheran faith, was helping
make hay at Lame Yost Yoder's. When he was asked to
pitch hay across from Little Crist, who drove the team,
Iasac said, "Well, today the work will be easy." Lame
Yost happened to hear him say it so in private Lame
Yost said to Little Crist, "Spunk up, Cristly. Show Isaac
that you can give him all he wants to do."

By four o'clock that hot afternoon in June, Isaac
said, "Cristly, I've got enough. I'll have to lie in the
shade a while. I hope your mother has onions sliced in
vinegar for supper. If she doesn't I can't go it any
longer." William enjoyed all these tales of strength and
endurance as the young fellows told them.

But he must not forget to ask about the things brother John and sister Margaret wanted to know about. One
evening when the work was done, Rosanna and Momly
were sitting on the high front porch plaiting straw to
make hats for the men. William approached and said,
"My brother John wants to know whether the Amish
people believe in hexing. He read in the *Public Ledger*
that they do."

"We know that it exists some places among the Pennsylvania German-speaking people," Momly admitted,
"but we do not practice it nor pay any attention to it. I
know of only one old Amish woman who was ever sus-
picioned, but nothing was ever done about it, and now
it has all been forgotten."

"Don't your people paint signs and symbols on your
barns and outbuildings to keep the hexes away?"

"No, we do not generally paint our barns at all. Some
people whitewash them but they must be plain white.
Signs and symbols would not be allowed by the church.

I have often heard that in Snyder County and in Berks County they believe in hexing, but none of our people live there."

"My sister Margaret read that when a family has a marriageable daughter they paint the front farm gate blue. Is that true?"

"No," said Momly, "we never announce anything about our boys and girls so far as marriage is concerned. They are completely free to choose whom they will. Our only wish is that they marry someone in our own church. To marry someone outside our church generally causes a good bit of trouble, and if they marry outside the Amish faith entirely they are excommunicated."

"And what does that mean?" asked William.

"When a person is excommunicated, his membership is taken away and we do not eat or drink with him. He dare not sit at the table with other members, but must eat alone till he is taken into the church again. You know the Bible says, 'With such do not eat,' and besides that we do not work with him or accept anything from him."

"That's pretty severe, isn't it?"

"Yes, but it is the best way to bring them to repentance," said Momly, somewhat sadly.

"Do the Amish believe in powwowing to stop pain and bleeding?"

"Yes, indeed," said Momly. "Many of our people can powwow not only to stop pain and bleeding but also to cure *Roth Lafe* (bilious chills), the take-off in children, wildfire (erysipelas), and *Püscht Bloder* (inflamed eyeball)."

"How is it done?"

"There are several different ways, but they are all based on the Bible. Everything is done in the name of the Father."

"I am learning to powwow," said Rosanna, "and already I can stop bleeding and take away pain, and Crist King is teaching me to cure wildfire. His way is very good. When Dr. Bigelow had the wildfire so bad and didn't get better, he finally sent for Crist King. Crist powwowed for him. The first day he was much better, and the second day he was just about well, and Dr. Bigelow didn't believe in powwowing either. He said powwowing was just an old woman's notion. But Crist King cured him when he was so bad the doctors couldn't do anything for him. I guess he will be a little more careful how he talks now."

William and Momly talked on and on. She told him all about his father, Patrick McGonegal, and his mother, Bridget O'Connor, when they began housekeeping in the Half Moon Valley. As she told about these things, William could faintly remember the little home where he was born, Reuben Kauffman taking them to the railroad station, and what his father said when Reuben refused to take money for bringing them to the station. ("I am sorry to leave these Amish people; they are so kind when one needs help.") When Rosanna told him that Reuben Kauffman lived near by William said, "I'll have to go to see him before I leave."

"Now, William, tell me about my sister, Margaret," Rosanna begged.

"Rosanna, you'll be proud of your sister Margaret when you see her. She's a beautiful young woman, tall and graceful with lovely manners. She attended St. Mary's Academy for three years, and is quite well educated. At present she is assistant librarian in the academy and that's a fine position."

"Momly and I planned that I would be a teacher, but later we thought best to change," said Rosanna with a touch of pathos in her voice which William noticed but he thought best not to ask any questions.

The most unusual experience for William came on Sunday when he went to preaching with the family. He sat on the front seat of the carriage with the bishop so that he could see the homes and the fields and the people more plainly as they drove. Reuben Kauffman took William with him into the house. Although William could not understand anything that was said, the somber attire of the people, their deep spirit of devotion, the great volume of the chorale singing, and the rhythmic flow of the German preaching reminded him somewhat of his own church and challenged his deepest reverence and devotion.

When preaching was out William was invited to share in the regular preaching dinner. He enjoyed the home-made oven-baked bread, the apple pies, the moon pies, the coffee, and the hot bean soup. After dinner, as he looked at the group of men standing in the yard, he thought he had never seen so many men with beards, and broadbrimmed hats, and somber clothes as he saw that day standing about talking quietly.

Some of the men he recognized from the harvest field at Bishop Shem's and he was pleased that many of them came and talked pleasantly with him. And when others learned that he was Rosanna's brother from Philadelphia they gathered around curiously to hear the fluent speech of this young man from the big city. They were pleased to hear him speak well of their beautiful mountains, the fertile fields and the abundant harvest. They took it as a compliment to their hard work and thrift.

During the last few days of William's stay, he and Rosanna talked a great deal about their personal affairs. William told her of his plan to own and manage a large department store in Philadelphia some day. He confided to her that he hoped to marry Mary McCarthy. "She is a beautiful young woman," William said. "After we are married I want you to come and stay with us a while, just as long as you like."

Then William asked Rosanna whether she had any definite plans for her life. Rosanna, feeling that it was right to confide in one's brother, told William about Little Crist Yoder, what a fine young man he was, and that they had never considered marrying anybody but each other. "Crist's father would like to divide his farm and would like Crist to take part of it. If everything works out now as planned, we may be married in January. I wish you could come to our wedding. An Amish wedding is a big affair." Rosanna had never even told Momly about their plans but she felt she should confide in William as her brother.

The day of William's departure arrived all too soon. Bishop Shem suggested that he had some business in Lewistown and thought it would be nice if Rosanna and Momly would go along and they would take William to meet his train. Nothing could have suited Rosanna better, for she had some important business in Lewistown too.

While Momly and Rosanna took William to the train, Bishop Shem attended to his business affairs. Momly had no fear this time that William would try to kidnap Rosanna as he had before. William had been so polite and thoughtful in her home that she really wanted to show him her deep appreciation by going to the train with him. William thanked Momly for her hospitality and told them both good-by. Then he boarded his train, and in a few minutes was lost to sight where the Blue Juniata winds through the foothills of the Alleghenies.

On the way to pick up Bishop Shem, Rosanna told Momly about her plan to marry Little Crist in January, if Momly agreed. And if Momly would give her consent she would buy her wedding dress today, as Lewistown was the place to buy dress material. Momly wasn't really surprised at this announcement. She had been hearing about Lame Yost dividing his farm. That meant that somebody would likely get married, and everything pointed to Little Crist and Rosanna.

"Well," said Momly, "Little Crist is one of the best young men in the valley. If you wish to get married I have nothing against it."

On the way home the Bishop was unusually jolly. When Momly asked him what made him feel so good, he said, "I have just had a great honor shown me and the Amish people today. I needed three hundred dollars to pay for some fattening steers this fall. When I asked lawyer Culbertson whether he would lend me the money, he said, 'Yes, sir, with pleasure.' And when I said, 'Fill out a note for six months and I'll sign it,' what do you think he said to me? He said, 'Bishop Yoder, I do not want your note. Your word is just as good as your bond to me. Pay me back whenever you are ready. I have learned that you Amishmen who wear hooks and eyes on your clothes never borrow more than you can pay back, and when you say you will pay it, you never fail to keep your word.' What do you think of that?"

"Der Herr sie gedankt" (Thank the Lord), said Elizabeth. "We will not fail him."

"Now, Rosanna, since pap has told us what makes him feel so good, don't you think you ought to tell him what makes you feel so good?"

"Yes, I'll tell him. I bought a wedding dress today."

"Well, that is news, now isn't it?" he said, laughing more heartily than usual. "If Little Crist Yoder is the lucky man, I give my consent gladly."

"But you must not tell anybody," said Rosanna.

"I'll not tell anybody but Momly," said Shem, and then Momly laughed, which was rather unusual. On the way home the white top carriage could hardly carry its load of happiness.

CHAPTER 11

The Wedding

FOR the remainder of the summer, time sped rapidly for Rosanna. Of course she would help Momly do all the fall work, clean the house and the yard and the garden, make soap, boil apple butter, and do the daily chores as usual, for if she changed the program in the slightest degree, some keen-minded Amish woman would sense "something in the wind," and Rosanna's secret would soon be known to everybody. The only visible sign of her intentions was the fact that Momly's flock of turkeys was a little larger than usual. Even Leah was not told of the plans. When Rosanna was making her wedding dress and Leah hinted at a wedding, Rosanna replied disinterestedly, "I've been needing a new dress this long time. I'm just getting one ready for winter."

During November and December, at least eight couples in Bishop Shem's congregation were married. People teased Rosanna and Little Crist and said, "Look out now. You'll be next." Crist just shook his head sadly and said, "Not for a while yet. Times are too hard to get married now." So well did he play his part, putting a little touch of regret into his voice, that even his closest friends said, "Doesn't look as though Crist and Rosanna are going to get married this winter."

But Rosanna and Momly were busy making plans secretly. They decided that Thursday, January the twenty-first, was to be the wedding day. Amish custom required them to be published (have their marriage announced at the close of preaching service) two Sundays before. They would be published on Sunday, January tenth.

When Little Crist came to see Rosanna now, he no longer announced his arrival with a few grains of corn. When he saw that all were in bed except Rosanna, who awaited him in the kitchen by the light of a tallow candle, he stepped quietly to the door and went in. They had a lot of things to talk about now—the date of the wedding; who would be Crist's *Schteckleimann* (a minister acting as a go-between in presenting a formal proposal for marriage); who the waiters would be; who would be the *Schnützler* (carver); where the marriage service would be held; and how many would be invited to the wedding.

When Rosanna told Little Crist that she and Momly had chosen January the twenty-first, Thursday, as the wedding day, Crist thought a few minutes and then said, "That will suit me fine. By that time we will have all our wheat hauled to market, the summer wood cut and hauled home, and the logs hauled to the sawmill to make posts and lumber. I want to get all this work done so pap and Eli will not have so much to do when I am gone."

When the holiday season was over, it was high time that Little Crist arrange for his *Schteckleimann* to go secretly to see Bishop Shem and Momly and get their consent to his marrying Rosanna. A young man usually chooses the minister whom he likes best of his own congregation. The minister whom Little Crist liked best was Crist L. Yoder. Little Crist went over to see Crist L. in the evening just before Crist L. went to bed. No one must know about this; so he went as late as he dared. This mission is always sort of an awkward affair for a young man. Little Crist was not surprised, when he called Preacher Crist out and told him why he was there that Crist L. laughed a bit—good-naturedly, of course.

The next evening Preacher Crist went over to Bishop Shem's house just a little before their bedtime. When he entered Sam and the girls had already gone to bed. After a few minutes of conversation, he said, "I have been asked by Yost Yoder's son Christian to come here and ask you folks whether you would be willing to give him your foster daughter, Rosanna McGonegal, in marriage."

The bishop spoke first. "He is an obedient member of the church, a good worker, is liked by everybody, and I believe he would make any girl a good husband. I have nothing against it."

After a moment's silence, Momly said, "I feel the same way," and the matter was settled.

Next evening Preacher Crist went over to Lame Yost's house, called Little Crist out, and said, "I have been to see Bishop Shem and Elizabeth and they are both willing to let you marry Rosanna."

Little Crist thanked him and said, "We have chosen Thursday, January the twenty-first, for our wedding day. Will you see to it that we are published on Sunday, the tenth? That will be two Sundays before the wedding." Preacher Crist said he would.

When Little Crist came into the room again, Sarah asked, "And what did Preacher Crist want?"

"He wants me to help them saw wood next week," said he, never batting an eye.

"I guess," answered Sarah with a suspicious little laugh.

Little Crist's next job was to buy some gray material for his wedding suit and take it to Franey Yoder, who was expert in making clothes for Amishmen. She was especially good at making a man's *Muhtze* (moot-sa—a coat something like a cutaway without a rolling collar, made with hooks and eyes). It was the required wedding garment for a young man. As he had not been published yet, Franey rolled her wise old eyes, but kept discreetly quiet. She was not going to lose her business through too much talking.

When Sunday the tenth came, Little Crist put on a brave front and went to preaching as usual. The boys noticed that he tied his horse where he could make an easy getaway. When he joined a group of young men, big Ben Sharp said, *"Well, heit, denk Ich gebts mohl epes"* (Today, I guess, there'll be something doing), and when Crist put on his most innocent look and inquired innocently what was going to happen, Ben laughed and said *"Der Gaul is hendig"* (Your horse is convenient).

Little Crist thought preaching services were never quite so long as that Sunday. He felt, too, that all eyes were on him, and yet nobody knew anything about it except those pledged not to reveal the secret. Finally, when the main sermon was ended, the prayer read, the benediction pronounced, all were seated and everybody listened almost breathlessly. This is the time when couples to be married soon are published by the deacon. When the place for the next preaching service was announced, Deacon John Hostetler said very slowly, as though teasing the congregation a bit by keeping the news from them as long as possible, "It has come to pass that a brother and a sister have agreed to enter the bonds of matrimony, namely, Yost Yoder's Christian and Rosanna McGonegal."

The minute this announcement was finished, Little Crist arose, went out, got his horse, and drove off to Bishop Shem's house as fast as he could go. Rosanna was awaiting him, for a girl never goes to preaching on the Sunday she is published. This was the first time Little Crist ever went to see her in the daytime. No more secrecy now. He and Rosanna were published. Everybody knew. On this special day he ate dinner with Ro-

sanna and a few chosen friends. Later when the bishop
and Momly came home from preaching, he visited with
them a while. All shyness was gone now.

When preaching was out and the girls were talking,
Sarah said, "Well, when I saw that Rosanna was not at
preaching today, I was just sure that she and Crist
would be published. But he was pretty sly about it. Now
I know that he is not going over to Crist L.'s next week
to saw wood, the little fibber. I thought he was fibbin'
when he told me. Crist L. was his *Schteckleimann*, I'll
bet you a dollar."

The next big job for Crist and Rosanna and Momly
was to decide whom they would invite to the wedding.
First of all, Little Crist's uncles, aunts, and cousins had
to be invited. Since Rosanna had no kinfolks in the valley, Momly and Bishop Shem's near relatives were invited instead. Then there was a host of Crist and Rosanna's young friends who were not related. When they
finally had the list completed, they found it contained
more than two hundred names.

"Well," said Momly, "the house is big. We have
plenty of turkeys and chickens and ham and beef, and
we can easily bake enough bread and pies and cakes.
We have lots of canned fruit and apples in the cellar.
Rosanna is a good girl and she must have a nice wedding."

"*Jah, well, Ich bins zufreide*" (All right, I am satisfied), said Bishop Shem.

Written invitations are not used. It was Little Crist's
job as bridegroom to drive around for the next week
and personally invite the two hundred people to his
wedding. Many were anxious to know just who was invited to the wedding. When women would meet each
other, one would say to the other, "*Host du en Stühle
an die Hochzüch?*" (Do you have a little stool to the

wedding? Literally, a stool to sit on at the wedding feast).

For the next ten days considerable effort was put forth to get ready for the wedding, for an Amish wedding is a large affair. The house was cleaned thoroughly and the tinware polished. The floors were scrubbed with silver sand to make them immaculately white. Temporary tables were built and everything tidied up in general. A number of men and women came to help to get the turkeys and chickens ready and bake the pies and bread and cakes a day or two before the wedding.

On the wedding day these same persons came again, early, to roast the turkeys and the chickens and fry the ham. They put up the temporary tables and set them as soon as the food was ready. These temporary tables were placed around three sides of the living room, the downstairs bedroom, the dining room. One table was set up in the kitchen. There were ten tables, each from fifteen to twenty feet long—enough to accommodate two hundred guests. Of course, the best food was placed on the "corner table," the table occupied by the bridal party.

While the hostess and twenty-five helpers were getting ready the noon meal, or wedding feast, the bride and groom and all the invited guests were at an Amish neighbor's house, where the marriage services would be held.

The marriage service was practically the same in order as a regular preaching service. The house was filled with benches as usual, and the bridal party sat on two rows of chairs facing each other, the boys in one row, the girls in the other, close to where the bishop and the minister stood while preaching.

When the first hymn was announced, the ministers headed to an upstairs room prepared for them. The whole bridal party followed to the stair door. Here the two young men "waiters" and the two young women "waiters" took seats provided for them while the bride and groom followed the bishop and the ministers to the upstairs council room. Here the bishop and the ministers instructed the ones to be married in the ethics of Christian marriage—the husband's duty to his wife and the wife's duty to her husband.

When this instruction was finished, the bride and groom returned downstairs. When they reached the stair door, the best man and his partner led the way to their regular seats while the bride and groom and the other couple followed. The singing by the congregation continued until the ministers returned from the upstairs room. Then the singing ceased and the minister speaking first stood up. He spoke for some twenty minutes and then all kneeled in silent prayer except the bridal party who stood facing their chairs. After the prayer everyone stood while the regular Scripture was read and then they sat down. The bishop preached the regular wedding sermon consisting of long passages of Scripture quoted verbatim from the Bible. These passages are chosen to portray home life and social life and are intended as instruction in proper living. This is a standard sermon and is preached at every wedding. At a certain point in the sermon, about twelve o'clock, the bishop reached the Bible incident where the servant of Tobias casts a net into the water, catching a fish having a golden ring in its mouth, which Tobias sends to his betrothed.

When this incident had been told, the Bishop said, "We have before us a brother and a sister who have agreed to enter the bonds of holy matrimony, namely, Christian Yoder and Rosanna McGonegal. If there is any brother or sister present who can give good cause why these two should not be married, let him speak now, for after this no complaint will be heard." The bishop paused a moment, and hearing no objections,

said, "There being no objection, you may present yourselves for marriage."

Little Crist and Rosanna then joined right hands and
were married in much the same way as couples in other
denominations marry. The services were closed with
testimony from ministers and deacons present, a few
more words from the bishop, a prayer from the prayerbook, the benediction, and the closing hymn. When the
hymn ended, the bridal party stood up first. The girls
put on their wraps and the boys their overcoats. They
met at the front door and proceeded to the front gate
where hostlers had brought the three buggies driven by
the groom and his two "best men." The bridal party and
all invited guests headed to the bride's home for the
wedding dinner.

About one o'clock, when everyone had arrived, Bishop Shem stepped to the door and announced, "Dinner is
now ready." He then directed the guests where to sit.
First, the bridal party was seated at the corner table,
from which they could see everybody and everybody
could see them. The bridal party sat behind the table
along the wall—Rosanna to the right side of the corner
and Little Crist to the left. The best man and his partner
sat next the groom and the other couple next the bride.
Next the unmarried girls filled in back of the table along
the wall around three sides of the room, while the unmarried young men sat facing the girls on the opposite
side of the table, their backs to the hollow square. The
young and middle-aged married women then took their
places, next the wall, around three sides of the table in
the dining room. The young husbands, especially the
singers, sat with their backs to the hollow square facing
the women. In similar manner the older men and
women sat at a table set up in the bedroom or at one in
the kitchen.

Rosanna and Crist waited patiently while Bishop

Shem directed the guests where to sit, not individually but by groups. When all were seated, the bishop took his seat at a convenient place at the singers' table in the dining room, paused a moment and then said, "If we are all seated, let us pray." Then all bowed their heads in silent prayer.

For the noon meal they had roasted turkey, stewed chicken, fried ham, mashed potatoes, sweet potatoes, bread, butter, apple butter, jellies, pies, and cakes. Although an Amish wedding dinner is not exactly a religious meal, it is always very orderly. A little fun for the bridal party is traditionally provided by the *Schnützler,* a young man who is a close friend of the bride and groom. He carves the turkey on the corner table and sees to it that the bridal party is well served.

The *Schnützler* for Rosanna and Little Crist was Dixie Dave Yoder, so called because he had done some traveling in the South. He was a jolly fellow and a good conversationalist. When he had served Little Crist a large piece of exquisite turkey, he said, "Remember, Cristly, how well I'm serving you today. When once you keep a house, I'll be in for dinner, and then you serve me as I'm serving you and Rosanna today."

"Bring your turkey with you," said Crist, "and I'll do it."

When the people were about through eating, Reuben Kauffman announced the first hymn, *Wacht auf, ruft uns die Stimme* (Awake, the Voice Is Calling Us). This hymn is always sung first after a wedding dinner and is very difficult, but Reuben was equal to the occasion. Wedding guests generally take their own singing books with them, a small book of German hymns. Since every body had a hymnbook and all loved to sing the wedding hymns, the great volume of unison singing, as was the custom in Germany over two hundred years ago, filled the house with melody and all hearts with joy and glad-

ness. When the sound of this great chorale died away,
pleasant conversation was resumed. Then Yost Yoder,
Bishop Shem's son, the singer, announced *Fröhlich
pfleg ich zu singen*, and the visiting ceased. As he began
with a strong voice with a fine tremolo in it, everyone
joined in heartily. Those who had served as cooks in the
kitchen came crowding to the doors of the room where
the singers sat. Others stood behind the men in the hollow square and raised their voices with the others in an
impressive blending of religion and good will. Everybody sang except Little Crist and Rosanna—brides and
grooms never sing on their wedding day. They were
both good singers, having sung these great wedding
hymns many times. It was almost more than Rosanna
could bear, and some said that they thought they saw
her eyes moisten during some of the hymns.

The first three hymns are distinctly wedding hymns
and must be sung in their regular order. First, *Wacht
auf, ruft uns die Stimme* (Awake, the Voice Is Calling
Us); second, *Fröhlich pfleg ich zu singen* (Joyously Do
I Sing); and third, *Schücket euch ihr lieben Gästen*
(Adapt Yourselves, Beloved Guests).

Hymns and conversation alternated pleasantly till
about four o'clock when all the young folks arose from
the table and started for the barn. Sam knew what they
expected. He had swept the barn floor the day before
and had everything in readiness. It was a beautiful
sunny winter day so that the doors and windows were
left open much of the time. As they went to the barn
Rosanna said, "Why, this is a summer day instead of a
winter day. They say a nice day means much happiness.
I hope it comes true this time."

"We'll just make it come true," said Little Crist.

At the barn they played the regular party games:
Bingo, Skip to Ma Lou, There Goes Topsy Through the
Window, O-Hi-O, and Six-Handed Reel. Crist and Ro-

sanna joined in heartily, for they knew that according to custom this was their last chance. Married people rarely if ever take part in party games, although it is not forbidden by the church. They seem to feel that when you are married you have joined the older folks and should leave the playing to younger ones.

As soon as the young folks went to the barn, the cooks came to clear off the table, wash the dishes, and reset the tables for supper. Much that remained from dinner was left on the tables for supper since not nearly everything was eaten. For fear there might be a shortage, Momly reinforced the meat supply with roast beef and dried beef, replenished the bread and cake plates, and added stewed and canned fruit.

When darkness began to fall, Reuben Kauffman was sent to the barn to tell the young folks to come to supper. At dinner the girls sat back of the table and the boys on the opposite side, but at the supper table all boys must have a partner and sit with her. The boys must take a girl in to the table whether they want to or not. Young married men enjoy standing at the door till every fellow has found a partner. If any young man pretends to be too timid to ask a girl, the married men bring him to the door forcibly. At the same time they grab a girl by the hand and send these two in together. After they are inside, all resistance ceases and together they go to the table. The facts are that these young fellows want to take a girl to the table, but it is not considered proper to seem anxious to do it; so they act timid and bashful.

With the exception of the young folks, the seating at the supper table was about the same as at noon. During the eating there was lots of lively conversation. When they had finished their supper, Ben Sharp announced a hymn of the slow chorale type, and once again the singing rose to inspiring volume. This time, however, no special hymns are required by custom. After two or three of the slow chorales had been sung Siever Yoder announced, *Wo ist Jesus mein Verlangen?* (Where Is Jesus, My Desired One?). From there on more and more of the selections were sung to "fast tunes."

At suppertime, wine was provided. Bottles of wine were placed here and there on the table, for was not wine served at wedding feasts in Bible times? While many took a sip of wine, nobody ever drank heavily. (Later, when temperance began to be advocated, the custom of serving wine at Amish weddings was discontinued.)

The wine was the medium of many jokes. If between hymns one wished to crack a joke to someone's mild embarrassment, he put a little wine in his glass, held it high and said, *"Es güld dem Hoch zeiter, wo er die Leder vergesse hot"* (A toast to the bridegroom when he forgot to take the ladder away from the window). All who knew the joke would laugh heartily. Eli had told Lewis Riehl that Crist had put a ladder to his window to slip out the first night he went courting and forgot to remove it, and Lewis sprung the toast. When someone proposed a toast in this fashion, nobody drank wine except the person proposing the toast, and in this way toasting did not lead to hilarity.

Later in the evening Little Crist held his glass high with a bit of wine in it and said, *"Es güld dem Lewis Riehl wo er eikschlofe is in der Gemeh"* (How about the time Lewis Riehl fell asleep during church?). Everybody laughed uproariously, for all remembered when Lewis had been out rather late one Saturday night, went to sleep in preaching next day, and fell off the bench on which he was sitting. Yost Yoder, the singer, toasted Ben Sharp for the time he got the wrong girl as he was leaving a Sunday evening's singing. So there was lots of fun at Rosanna's wedding, for many good friends had gathered to do her honor around heavily laden tables seating two hundred people.

When things were at their height, four men who had served as cooks came in with long-handled pewter or brass dippers to take up a collection for the cooks. As coins were dropped into the dippers, the men shook them vigorously making all the clatter possible, letting everyone know how hard they had worked to prepare the fine meal, how poor they were, and how much they needed the money. If someone pretended not to hear or to be unwilling to give, they shook their dippers at his ears with such terrific din that he was glad to throw in a coin.

Siever Yoder passed the dipper at the corner table, and when he came to the bridegroom, Little Crist ignored him. Then Siever shook the dipper as noisily as possible and said, "Oh, Little Crist, look what a fine dinner and supper we have prepared for you. Think, O Bridegroom, how we slaved that you might eat this day like a king. Have mercy on us poor men and women and give freely of your unbounded wealth. Set a good example to these other banqueters that they may give freely, for all my brother cooks will bear witness that we sorely need the money." And the higher the flow of Siever's oratory, the louder the guests laughed, until finally Little Crist dropped a silver dollar into the bowl. This coin changed the tone of the rattling. Siever in make-believe gratitude bowed and thanked the bridegroom for his unlimited generosity.

In a new outburst of oratory Siever said, "Today we serve a noble man, a man of wealth, a man of generous disposition, a man who sympathizes with the cruel position of the poor, and with our humble hearts aglow with gratitude we thank you, good sir." Whatever was collected was divided among the twenty-five cooks and helpers, who used the money to buy some little souvenir by which to remember the pleasure they had at Rosanna's wedding. These cooks were all friends, who were in comfortable circumstances, but it was great sport to play the part of needy servants and extract money from their banqueting friends.

When the singing and the pleasantry had continued to near nine o'clock, the young folks arose from the table and went to the barn again, where they played the same kind of party games as in the afternoon. About eleven o'clock they returned to the house again in couples, nibbled a bit at the food and sang and joked as before. About one o'clock the bride and groom retired, and that was the signal that the wedding was over.

As they were leaving the table, Reuben Kauffman, who had known Rosanna from her babyhood in Half Moon Valley and who had always taken a keen interest in her welfare, remembered that he had helped Rosanna and Little Crist get together at her first cornhusking. He looked admiringly at the bride and groom and said, "My, what a beautiful match! She is a black-eyed, Irish brunette, and he is a fair-haired, blue-eyed German blond, a perfect mating of opposites! What a pair!"

Rosanna's blue wedding dress and her white kerchief and apron seemed to enhance her red cheeks and bright eyes. Little Crist's gray suit, his slightly trimmed beard, his hair just as short as allowable, made him look every inch a man, even though he was small. Many a young fellow in that group knew the iron of his muscles in wrestling and had great respect for his strength.

Before going to their room, Rosanna said, "Let's look at the wedding presents." One of the bedrooms upstairs had been set apart for presents. Waiting for them on the bed, on the bureau, on the chest, and even on the floor were the tokens of love and friendship—dishes, lamps, tablecloths, towels, clocks, handkerchiefs, saws, hatchets, hammers, wrenches, and even an ax for Little

Crist. Probably the most beautiful present came from
Philadelphia, a linen table cloth from John and William
and Margaret. Rosanna, her eyes dimmed with gratitude, said to Cristly, "My, isn't it nice to have good
friends! In the years to come we'll prove to them that
we were worthy of these beautiful gifts, won't we?"

As the cooks began to clear away the food and as the
temporary tables were taken down, the guests, somewhat weary now of feasting and jesting, began putting
on their shawls and bonnets and hats and coats. Good-
nights echoed throughout Momly's spacious house and
Rosanna's wedding was over. Amish weddings are all
like Rosanna's, except some are not quite so large.

CHAPTER 12

The Dower

THE second day after the wedding, Rosanna went
home with Crist to the big stone house where Lame
Yost and his wife Catherine lived. Rosanna had known
Crist's sisters, Sarah and Franey, for several years, but
she had never been in his home except on such formal
occasions as preaching or a singing. She had always
wanted to visit with Catherine, his mother, for she
seemed such a kindly person, but custom simply did not
allow it. She wondered, too, what kind of man Lame
Yost was. He looked rather stern, but his voice was low
and it had a musical note in it that attracted strangers
and inspired confidence.

Lame Yost was not a fluent talker, but Rosanna
thought as she spoke to him on her first visit that she
detected a note of appreciation, which made her feel
very much at home. Crist's mother was more talkative,

and it was not long till she and Rosanna visited quite comfortably. Eli, the younger son, was a bit timid at first, but the girls with their many mutual interests made Rosanna feel very welcome and at home right from the first.

As Rosanna looked about the large well-furnished house, the well-spread table, and the signs of plenty everywhere, she could not help but have a deep feeling of satisfaction that she had been privileged to cast her lot with a family like that—highly respected by everybody, in good standing in the church, comfortable in material things, and above all, happy and content in each other's presence.

A few days after the wedding festivities Rosanna said to Little Crist, "For the next few weeks we will have to visit all our uncles and aunts and cousins. You know they will expect us."

When the first week end approached, they went over to spend the night at Uncle Christian's. He was known as "Charley Crist," because one night before he was married, he went on horseback to see Solmy. As he crossed a wooden bridge near her home, he said to the horse, *"Schleich, Charley, schleich"* (Sneak, Charley, sneak). Some boys happened to hear him, and ever after he was called "Charley Crist."

Solmy was a gracious mother, and she welcomed the newlyweds most heartily so that if at any time they felt any timidity, it was soon dispelled. What a supper awaited them—stewed chicken with waffles and gravy, candied sweet potatoes, creamed sweet corn, snow-white mashed potatoes, and all sorts of jellies, jams, cakes, and cookies. It was almost a second wedding dinner. Rosanna had never lacked anything, but this seemed like sheer luxury.

Sunday evening they went to Uncle Nicholas's, over by the front mountain. Here another feast was prepared. During the night Rosanna was awakened, she thought, by the cry of a wildcat or a panther reverberating along the mountainside. When daylight came, they looked out the window and saw in the orchard two full-grown deer. They had come down from the mountain and by pawing the snow away were able to eat the grass in the orchard.

Next night they went to Uncle Eli Zook's and so on until all the uncles and aunts and cousins had been visited. Little Crist said, "I wish we did not have to spend so much time visiting, but since that is the custom, we will have to do it. It will not be long now till spring, and I must be attending some sales and buying some farm machinery and horses. I don't want to be behind with my work when spring comes."

A month before the first of April, Lame Yost notified the man in his tenant house that he would have to move. This was merely a formality since Peter Anthony, the big strong German, knew very well that Little Crist would want the tenant house until his father had finished the new house and barn for him on the west division of the farm.

Rosanna knew that she did not have to live in the tenant house for long, so she did not move all her things in, but waited to move them in the fall when the new house and barn would be completed. The first summer Little Crist shifted along with as little machinery and as few horses as possible. When fall came, the real moving took place.

On the day they moved into the new house, there was considerable activity, both at Lame Yost's big stone house and at Bishop Shem's house. There was a hint of rivalry as to which household would contribute most to this young couple as they began farming in earnest. Shem's son, Sam, brought Rosanna's things up on the two-horse wagon, things which Momly and the bishop had given her to set up housekeeping. On the wagon was a table, a bureau, a cupboard, a stove, a bed, bed-clothing, a half dozen chairs with a rocker to match, and behind the wagon, a horse and harness, and the best cow in Bishop Shem's stable. Rosanna had been a good girl and a hard worker. She had helped in the harvest field, and at cornhusking. She had always been ready for every household duty. Now was the chance for Bishop Shem to show his appreciation; so he presented her with the best cow, besides chickens, hams, potatoes, and flour.

From the big stone house for Little Crist came a bed and bedding, a Windsor desk, a set of dishes, some handworked linen, a tablecloth, a horse and harness, a harrow and a cow, again the best in the herd. Do you think Lame Yost Yoder with his large farm, his big house and barn, his high financial rating in the community was going to give his oldest son a shabby horse or a worthless cow! When his horse ran away five years before throwing him from the carriage and breaking his leg, it had lamed him for life. Little Crist, then only sixteen, assumed the responsibility of the farm in such a manly way that nothing was lost in crops or cattle. Such a son deserved the best; so the horse was to be his own choice. Little Crist chose Harry, the big dapple gray Percheron gelding, weighing 1700 pounds and as beautiful as an Arabian stallion.

Setting up these young folks in housekeeping that fall was a real occasion. It was the delightful union of two families of high standing. Eli twitted Leah, and Sam teased Sarah and Franey. Lame Yost and Bishop Shem sat by smiling at the jokes and clever remarks bandied back and forth among the movers. Momly and Catherine busied themselves making the beds and arranging the dishes and the linens with hands whose every touch carried a blessing with it. Sometimes they did not utter a

word for a long time as tears moistened their eyes.
Momly was thinking of the little Irish baby she had
raised to womanhood, from whom she had never been
separated but must now give up. Catherine was thinking
of her first born, the son so dear to her mother heart
who must now leave her fireside. Of course, Rosanna
and Little Crist were not going far, but still they were
going. Today for the first time these two strong, pious
women felt that they had a very sacred common interest.

Sarah, Franey, and Leah made themselves responsible for preparing and cooking the dinner. When the
large platters of stewed chicken, fried ham, and mashed
potatoes had been put on the table together with all the
jams and jellies and gravies, Sarah went to the door and
said to Little Crist, "Call the men to dinner." When
they were ready to be seated, Little Crist said to Bishop
Shem, "Shem, you take the head of the table."

The bishop replied, "Oh, no, Cristly. Today you are
the man of the house, and the man of the house always
takes the head of the table."

Little Crist, taking his place at the head of the table,
smiled and said, "Will you all be seated?" After the silent grace was finished, Crist attempted to fill his new
role properly by saying, "Now, you must all reach and
help yourselves." That's what every Amishman is expected to say immediately after the blessing when there
are guests at the table.

It was a jolly meal in the large square kitchen in the
new house. Rosanna presided in a general way, but
Franey "chased the flies," Sarah attended to the water
and coffee, and Leah replenished the chicken and ham
platters when they got low. As they ate, Bishop Shem
volunteering a little pleasantry said, *"Well, Yoscht,
denks du die Kinner kenne houshalde?"* (Well, Yost, do
you think these children can keep house?).

Lame Yost pondered a minute and then countered, *"Well, wann du die Rosanna so gut ufgezoge host es Ich der Crist hab, glab Ich gehts"* (Well, if you raised Rosanna as well as I raised Crist, I believe it will go). Catherine smiled contentedly, for she felt her husband had given the bishop a pretty good answer.

When all had finished eating, Little Crist paused a moment, then all bowed their heads in a silent grace of thanksgiving for the meal. As they left the table the men lingered in the kitchen while the girls who had waited on the table ate their dinner. To show their gallantry, Eli and Sam served them. They made many blunders, some intentional, some unknowingly, as they served, but they justified themselves by saying that strong men are not supposed to do housework.

When the evening shadows deepened and the cricket's chirp echoed in the crisp October air, Little Crist and Rosanna sat alone by the kitchen stove reviewing all the activities of the day. Rosanna said, "Well, we have a lot of things to be thankful for. We have a new house and barn, two horses, two cows, a plow, a harrow, a table, a stove, a cupboard, two beds and bedding, plenty of quilts and blankets, a desk, a bureau, dishes and chairs, and about everything we need."

"You missed a very important item which I got," said Crist.

"What is it?" said Rosanna thoughtfully. "I thought I named everything."

Crist took her in his arms and said, "I got Rosanna McGonegal, the nicest girl in the world!"

CHAPTER 13

Keeping House

IT was not long till spring now, and Little Crist was busy going to sales and buying a few more horses and cows and some farming implements. His specialty was horses, and he said to his father one day, "If I see a horse that is offered cheap, I'll buy him, feed him up, sell him, and try to make some money."

"It's pretty risky business. You can't see inside of 'em and sometimes they are pretty weak," said his father. "But if you're careful, you may make a little."

Crist studied the horse doctor book diligently until he thought he knew a good deal about the age of a horse by his teeth and the location of the most common blemishes—ringbone, spavin, and eye weakness. He believed he could also tell a lot about a horse's constitution by the shape and position of his feet.

He heard that Nancy Jake Yoder had a horse to sell, but he also knew that Nancy Jake was about the shrewdest horsetrader in the whole valley. There could be no harm in looking at the horse, he decided. Nancy Jake lived along the back mountain, and when Crist went back to see him, Nancy Jake said, "Yes sir, Cristly, I have a horse to sell."

"Is he sound and all right?"

"I'll show you the horse. The buyer must be the judge."

Jake trotted the horse out, but Little Crist noticed that he limped slightly on his left hind leg. When the horse came to rest Crist examined his leg and said "Ringbone."

"Are you sure?" asked Jake.

"Well, he has a slight limp when he trots and he has a bit of enlargement above the pastern joint. He might do me for light work if I keep him off the road, but he's not worth much money. He may go bad at any time."

Jake blinked his wise old eyes and said, "You blasted little jockey. I didn't think you'd notice that, but you are right. I keep only first-class horses, so you may have this one for half price."

The deal was made. Crist took the horse home, laughing up his sleeve because he had learned how to cure ringbone, a secret very few men knew. If he cured this horse, he could sell him for a fine profit and Daddy Yost would smile. The cure was simple—the application of a salt and vinegar solution daily and thorough rubbing three times per day.

Crist applied the horse doctor book remedy vigorously and to his delight, after a month's treatment, he saw that the ringbone was considerably smaller. By midsummer the ringbone, as well as the limp, had entirely disappeared. Horses at that time of year were in heavy demand, and buyers were numerous. Dave Mutersbaugh, a horse buyer from Lewistown, stopped by one day and said, "Cristly, have you any horses to sell?"

"Oh, I have one or two I might sell if anybody wants them badly," said Crist nonchalantly.

"Trot 'im out," said Dave. Crist brought out the bay he had treated for ringbone. He was a beauty, had fine knee action, and as Crist trotted him up and down, Dave said, "Pretty nice horse. Is he sound?"

"So far as I know," said Crist.

"What do you want for him?"

"Two hundred dollars."

"Oh, you're too high!" Dave exclaimed.

"All right, if you don't know a good horse when you see one, nobody loses but you," said Crist, leading the horse back into his stall. Little Crist's indifference and what he had just said irked Dave considerably. After a bit more pressure from Dave during which Crist maintained his show of indifference, Mutersbaugh said, "I'll take him." He counted out ten twenty-dollar bills, and led the horse away.

Little Crist could hardly wait to get to the house to tell Rosanna how fortunate they were. He had bought a horse for one hundred dollars and sold him for two hundred, after keeping him only three months—one hundred dollars clear gain! Rosanna smiled and using a little Irish brogue said, "Little Crist Yoder, a schmart man it is that you air. Some day you'll be the horse king of the Kishacoquillas." He was pleased with her comment, especially with her last phrase, "horse king of the Kishacoquillas!"

Soon the field work began in earnest. Little Crist said to his wife one day, as they were eating dinner, "Rosanna, when we are working in the fields, ring the dinner bell at quarter after eleven and we'll unhitch at once and come home. If we are working about the barn, then ring the bell when dinner is ready and we'll come at once. If you always ring the bell when you have the meal ready, we will come at once, and will not lose any time. With this understanding both you and I can get our work done to the best advantage.

"Before we were married, I helped Jake Hartzler build fence one day. When Motley blew the dinner horn (the church they belonged to did not allow dinner bells), we went right on working for almost a half hour. When we finally got to the house, dinner had stood on the table and was cold. Motley was disgusted because the good dinner she had prepared with so much care wasn't at its best. I saw then how wrong it is for men to treat their wives that way. I made up my mind to treat my wife better if I ever had one. What do you think of the idea, Rosanna?"

"That suits me fine. Down at Bishop Shem's, Momly always blew the dinner horn ten minutes before dinner was ready. That gave the men time to get in and wash for dinner, but sometimes when Sam wanted to finish a job, he would go on working till he was through and come to dinner late. Momly never said much, but the bishop saw that it made things unhandy for the women folks: He finally told Sam that after that when the dinner horn blows, he shall drop his work at once and come to dinner and finish afterwards." So the agreement was made and carefully adhered to. When they sat down to a meal the food was always hot and inviting.

Rosanna was just as determined to get ahead as Little Crist was. The chickens were laying well, and the cows gave good milk. Rosanna was making two or three nice rolls of butter per week above their need. These she took to the store and the eggs and the butter more than paid for the groceries. She felt happy that she was keeping up her end of the housekeeping.

One day when Ann Roper came over from the village to buy some cream, she said, "My gracious, Rosanna! Don't you find this awful hard work—feeding chickens and pigs, cooking, and milking cows? Do you ever have time to play cards?"

Rosanna stopped polishing her tinware for a moment, turned and looked at Ann and said with a touch of pity in her voice, "No, Ann, I do not have time to play cards and I wouldn't play cards even if I had time. I think it is a waste of time. Besides, our church doesn't allow card playing. And this is not hard work. With a new house and barn, a sober, industrious husband, new furnishings in the house, beautiful horses to work and drive, and a chance to buy our farm when we wish, feeding chickens and pigs and making butter and cooking are not hard work. It's fun and pleasure and enjoyment!"

"Rosanna, I envy you. You're a happy woman. I wish I had your philosophy of life," said Ann, with a note of disappointment in her voice.

Rosanna was happy in her new home, but from the first she went to see Momly each week. When she knew that Momly had company, she frequently went down to help her. Even though Momly had always been a strong, healthy woman, she was beginning to age a bit. While she would never complain, work did not go quite so easily for her as in earlier years.

Momly frequently came up to spend the day with Rosanna, too. She loved Bishop Shem. Leah, his daughter, was kind to her. But she somehow felt that Rosanna was her own daughter. She had taken her as a little baby five days old and raised her to womanhood. Now to be separated from Rosanna was more of a burden to Elizabeth than she had expected. She never came to see Rosanna without bringing something for her in her basket.

One day in the early spring Rosanna looked out the window toward the barn and saw Momly coming under the "overshot" with her basket. Rosanna was so glad to see her again that she hurried out to meet her. When they came into the house, Momly took the covering off the basket and said, "I brought you a can of tomatoes and a can of sauerkraut," and then repeated "a can of tomatoes and a can of sauerkraut." When Rosanna seemed a bit worried about this soliloquy, Momly said, "I was just thinking. Long ago, one day over in Half Moon Valley I took your mother a can of tomatoes and a can of sauerkraut. Come to think of it, I carried them in this very basket. That was thirty years ago, before you were born. How pleased your mother was. I'll never forget her, so strong and beautiful. Had the doctor only

treated her right when you were born, we might have
her with us yet. But then I never would have had you.
The bishop sometimes says in his sermon, *'Wass Got
tuht ist wohl getahn'* (What God doeth is well done),
and I guess it is true."

As they sat and talked, Rosanna began to knit a little
stocking. A look of deep satisfaction brightened Momly's face, but she said nothing until she left for home.
Then she said, *"Wann du mich mohl brauchst, kum Ich"*
(When you need me, I'll come).

Rosanna and Little Crist were nearing the second
summer of housekeeping when their firstborn came.
The baby was a little boy, and according to custom, was
named after its paternal grandfather. Little Crist did not
want to be selfish, so he said, "Since your father is not
living, would you be willing to name our baby after my
father?"

"I am perfectly willing," said Rosanna, "and would
you be willing that his middle name be McGonegal?"
That, too, was an old custom and so the baby was
named Yost McGonegal Yoder. Baby Yost was the first
grandchild in both families; so he was very popular.
Lame Yost came frequently to see his little namesake,
and one day he said to Rosanna, *"Wann er mohl gross
genung is, kaff Ich ihm en paar Hosse"* (When he is big
enough, I'll buy him a pair of pants). At preaching,
Catherine and Momly vied with each other as to which
one was to hold the little newcomer.

Baby Yost grew well. When he was about a year and
a half old, a little sister joined the family. Little Yost
took great interest in her, but it was Rosanna who was
most pleased of all. Now she would have an opportunity
to honor Momly in the finest possible way. She would
name her little girl Elizabeth. How she had hoped the
second baby would be a little girl, so that she might
show Momly how grateful she was to her for all she had

meant to Rosanna. When Rosanna told her that she
would name the little girl Elizabeth for her, Momly
reacted with joy and happiness. Little Yost now had to
share the attention of Momly, but to Grandpa Yost, he
was still *the* boy.

With two little ones to care for, Rosanna found that
she would have to have help. In the community was a
middle-aged woman who had no home of her own. Rosanna asked her to come and help care for the children
and assist with the work. This woman was Mary Ann
Carson, a Scotch Irish Presbyterian. For many years she
kept house for John Armstrong but when Armstrong
died, she was without a home.

Mary Ann gladly came to help Rosanna. As she
worked in the home, she became much more than merely a housemaid. She became a friend.

And as the years passed, this friendship between Rosanna and Mary Ann ripened into a mutual dependence
so that when Mary Ann was out of work she always
knew that she was welcome at Rosanna Yoder's, and
there she would go for a week or a month and stay as a
kind of helping guest. She was an intelligent woman.
She spoke good English and understood Pennsylvania
German, but she refused to speak it. As a result, all of
Rosanna's children as they were growing up learned to
speak good English along with the Pennsylvania German. They were two-language children right from the
beginning.

Mary Ann liked little children. She became fond of
Little Yost as he followed her about trying to say one
English word after another. Baby Elizabeth smiled and
cooed and prattled as though she too were trying to
learn to speak English. All this was a great satisfaction
to Little Crist and Rosanna, for when they had occasion
to go away for an evening or to attend preaching in

stormy weather, they could leave the children with Mary Ann with perfect confidence.

By this time Little Crist was getting his farm well organized. He had to be away from home rather frequently now because he was buying and selling more horses. It was clear that if he wished to have the field work done in time and season, he needed a hired hand. The first one to work for him was Siever Yoder, whom he had known for many years. Since he knew Siever was reliable, he felt justified in buying and selling horses still more extensively.

Often in the fall of the year Little Crist would go over to Stone Valley to Hetty Porter's or Sam Powell's or Hiram Ross' across Broad Mountain and sometimes as far west as Ennisville or Neff's Mills. Sometimes he'd buy three or four horses on one trip. He knew that sometimes feed became scarce during the winter in Stone Valley and that he could buy horses cheaply.

One fall he went over to Hetty Porter's and said to her, "Hetty, have you any horses to sell?"

"Yes, I'll sell any horse in the stable. I have too many to keep over winter. Besides I need a little money to pay my taxes."

Crist walked into the stable and looked them over. He noticed a dapple brown, his favorite color, that had the makings of a fine horse. He had good large feet, straight, well-boned legs, was broad across the chest and between the ears, had large intelligent eyes and an honest-looking face.

"What'll you take for that horse, Hetty?"

"He's a good one," said Hetty. "I'll take one hundred and fifty dollars for him. He's worth more, but my grain is too scarce to keep him over winter."

Crist had schooled himself to bargain a bit, no matter what price was asked, but when Hetty said "one hundred and fifty dollars," for that fine horse, he did not have the nerve to offer less. He would have felt guilty of taking advantage of a woman when she had to sell, so he said enthusiastically, "Here's your money and I hope it will help you out."

Hetty's husband had been killed by the kick of a horse, and she was trying to raise her four boys and two girls on the farm. Crist had too much of the Golden Rule principle in his heart to press for the lowest price with a woman like that. As he bridled the horse and led him away, Hetty almost wept, but she managed to say, "I hope you have good luck with him, Cristly." Never had he bought a horse with such possibilities—five years old, as pretty as a picture and as sound as a dollar.

Little Crist called the horse Harry, after Hetty's oldest son, and he never went to the stable without the sight of Harry filling him with satisfaction. He said to Siever, "I want you to curry Harry thoroughly every day and if we work him, then twice a day." Crist fed the horses himself, for proper feeding is an art, and he assumed that responsibility himself.

By spring Harry had gained considerable weight and that together with Siever's currying made him a handsome horse indeed. When Siever led him out to water daily, Harry had the spirit of a mountain deer and the gentleness of a mother sheep. Crist reasoned that a horse with such a disposition would make a wonderful leader. He could hardly wait till spring farming came to hitch him in the lead, put a single line on him and teach him the meaning of "Gee" and "Haw." But Little Crist discovered someone had already taught him, for he was as much at home in the furrow as an old fire horse on the way to a burning building.

The more Crist worked Harry as a leader the better he liked him, and he mused, "I must keep that horse to stabilize my rapidly changing team. Harry will make any horse work beside him."

But one day Dave Mutersbaugh came along buying horses and as he entered the stable door he said, "I need a good horse. Have you any to sell, Cristly?"

"Yes sir, I'll sell any horse in the stable except the front one (that was Harry)."

Dave looked them all over and then said, "What's your price on that front horse?"

"He's not for sale," said Crist emphatically.

"Well, if you would sell him, what price would you ask?"

Finally Little Crist said, "Well, if any man would be fool enough to give me three hundred and fifty dollars for him, I guess I'd let him go."

"Sold!" said Mutersbaugh, and reached for his wallet.

"But," remonstrated Crist, "He's not for sale."

"Come on," said Dave. "You can't back out now. You said you'd take three hundred and fifty dollars for him and here's your money."

"I'm a man of my word," Crist replied, "and I said I'd take three hundred and fifty dollars for him, if any man was fool enough to give it. But Dave, I didn't class you in that crowd."

"Cristly, do you know why I gave it to you? I know a man who has five horses that look exactly like him. If I set this horse among them, you couldn't tell me which was your horse. He wants the sixth horse and he will give me five hundred dollars for this horse. One hundred and fifty dollars sure profit makes most any man a little foolish, eh, Cristly? That six-horse team will be worth five thousand dollars."

As Harry was led out the lane, he looked back and whinnied as if he were trying to say, "Good-by, master. I'm sorry to leave you." Little Crist Yoder almost wept.

Afterwards, when talking about Harry, Crist would say somewhat regretfully, "That horse could almost talk English. I know he understood it, for no matter how far away he was, if I told him to come to me, he would come. If I told him to go forward three steps, he went. If I told him to turn to the right or to the left, he did so willingly. Yes sir, that horse could almost talk English. If I ever buy another like him, I'll not sell him for any money. Horses like that just seem to bless your stable with peace and prosperity."

CHAPTER 14

Margaret's Visit

ROSANNA'S butter and egg production was increasing more and more. Her cows gave a fine grade of milk. Her springhouse, through which a fresh limestone spring flowed in a constant stream, was so cold that butter and milk were kept sweet for the longest possible time. This enabled Rosanna to make a fine quality of solid butter, which was eagerly sought by the nearby townsfolk.

Butter was selling anywhere from ten to twenty-five cents per pound, and when dealers came to buy butter and took fifteen to twenty-five pounds at a time it was bothersome to get a pencil and paper each time and figure out the amount. She knew that some of them were not above making slight "errors," always in their own favor. Rosanna had an idea. She noticed on the back of an almanac a sort of pyramid multiplication table which went as far as twenty-four times twenty-four. She decided to memorize the entire table so that when someone bought seventeen pounds of butter at nineteen cents a pound, instead of getting a pencil to figure it out she could say offhand seventeen times nineteen is three hundred twenty-three, or three dollars and twenty-three cents. She enjoyed the mental exercise of learning the table.

She had gotten as far as the twenty-first line when little Crist came home from town one day with a letter postmarked in Philadelphia. She opened it eagerly and unfolded a letter from her sister Margaret. Margaret was coming to see her in July! For years they had been corresponding now and then, but Rosanna had a deep desire to see and know Margaret, her only sister.

Rosanna replied at once expressing her great delight. She assured Margaret that she awaited her visit with great anticipation and pleasure. She asked Margaret to let her know the day she would arrive so that someone might meet her at Reedsville and spare her the lumbering stagecoach ride to Belleville. About the middle of July another letter came saying Margaret would arrive Thursday evening, July twenty-four.

When the day arrived, there was real excitement around the Yoder house. Little Crist hitched his fastest horse to his yellow top carriage and drove to Reedsville to meet the four o'clock train. He wanted to be there early to give the horse a bite to eat, a drink of water, and a short rest so that the trip back home could be made as fast as possible.

When the train arrived at Reedsville, Little Crist was on the platform looking for someone whom he had never seen. Only three ladies got off the train. He knew one of them, Mrs. Rice, the grain merchant's wife. The other two looked more like shoppers than travelers, but he stepped up to these ladies and inquired, "Are either of you ladies Margaret McGonegal?" When they both replied, "No sir," he hardly knew what to do. That was the last train of the day from the east, so all he could do was drive home and tell Rosanna that Margaret did not come. Rosanna was greatly disappointed, but she consoled herself with the thought that Margaret was a woman of affairs and if she missed connections at Harrisburg, as doubtless she had, Margaret could take care of herself for the night.

Next day there was no message, but Rosanna had a feeling that Margaret would arrive on the stagecoach that evening. She set her house in order, washed and dressed little Yost and Elizabeth, put on her own good dress, and awaited the arrival of the stagecoach about six-thirty. When the time drew near, she could scarcely wait. She watched and she listened and just a minute after six-thirty she heard a heavy vehicle rumble over the wooden bridge a quarter mile down the bend of the road and around the low hill. "Oh, that must be the stage," she thought. In another minute she heard the familiar clatter of the horses' feet, and then the stage appeared with the horses in a fast trot. That must be Margaret, but she waited till the horses swung in towards the outer gate and stopped.

Then she saw a woman dressed in black alight from the stage and heard her ask, "In this road?" Rosanna could wait no longer. She hurried out the lane to meet the visitor still wondering in her heart whether this really was her sister. When they met face to face, there was no doubt. Margaret threw her arms around Rosanna and said, "My sister!" and for a moment both were so overcome that neither could speak. When the first wave of emotion subsided, they seemed to look at each other for unmistakable signs of family resemblance. Margaret was taller, but both had black wavy hair, dark brown eyes, red cheeks, and rather dark complexions.

Margaret spoke first. "I kept thinking as I came, maybe this is not my sister after all, but there is no mistake. We are both as Irish as St. Patrick himself. God bless the Irish!"

As they walked in the lane, Rosanna told how Crist had been to Reedsville to meet her the day before and when she did not come, how worried they were for fear something might have happened to her. Then Margaret told her the trains missed connection at Harrisburg and how she had to stay there over night. "They told me," said Margaret, "that this connection is often missed as it is very close. They assured me that I would have no trouble today, and I had no difficulty finding my way out here."

When they reached the house, Margaret was charmed with the chubby-cheeked children. While she faintly remembered the Amish in Half Moon Valley, she had forgotten that little boys are dressed like miniature Amishmen—with long pants and the same cut of coat, hair, and hat as daddy's. When she saw three-year-old Yost with his long pants, broadbrimmed hat, little white muslin shirt, and no suspenders her amusement almost overcame her delight. As Margaret looked at him she said, "Even though he has a big hat and long hair, you can't hide the Irish in him." Little Elizabeth, just learning to walk, was wearing a little white cap, a pink dress, and long apron (a sort of pinafore). Margaret found her quaint and adorable.

When Margaret met Little Crist, she recalled Reuben Kauffman back in Half Moon Valley. She was only seven years old when they left that valley, but she remembered Momly and how kind she was to the children in the great sorrow of losing their mother. She wanted to see Elizabeth again. (Margaret remembered her as Elizabeth; it was Rosanna who gave her the name Momly.)

Even though Margaret had known Amish folks when she was a little girl, the sight of all these men and women in their quaint garb made her feel that she was in a foreign country. The men were all rugged looking, but as she looked at them more closely, she noticed that they had fine complexions, clear skin, and red cheeks. While the men all wore beards, they shaved the upper lip and the upper part of the cheek so that their complexions often showed off to good advantage.

The women all wore white caps and dresses made of perfectly plain material without ruffle or lace. Their cap-encircled faces, because of so much outdoor work, carried a deep tan which city ladies often coveted. What impressed Margaret was the fact that everyone bore the stamp of health and strength. She observed no intoxication, no poverty, nobody destitute among them. Such equality and such uniformity she had never seen before: None of the Amish were rich and none were poor. In cut of garment there was absolute uniformity; in color, variety. Margaret noticed that these plain people were not only modest in their dress but in their speech as well. Most of them spoke in short sentences and in low tones and were rather reluctant to talk with outsiders.

Margaret had lived in the city ever since she was a little girl. The pure clean air, the unobstructed sunshine, the abundant foliage of the trees, the delightful freshness of the fruits and vegetables on the table, and the aroma of the country-cured ham filled her with wonder and delight. Little Crist had a fine field of second-crop clover in full bloom. Margaret walked through it every day and filled her lungs and her soul, as she said, with the rich perfume of that beautiful field.

This was blackberry season, too. One day they all went to the mountain to pick blackberries. Margaret thought blackberries grew on trees. When she found that she could walk up to a bush and pick off and eat all she wanted with perfect freedom, she was thrilled. At first she was afraid and asked Little Crist, "Are you sure that there are no bear or alligators in these bushes?" Crist was tempted to tell her that there were no alligators but she had better keep a firm lookout for whale and buffalo, but not wishing to make fun of her, he answered her truthfully. In a surprisingly short time Rosanna and Crist had gathered three large buckets of blackberries. When Margaret saw them carry these buckets filled with perfect berries, she thought she had never seen such abundance before. In the city one had to pay for every berry, and here you carried them away in bucketfuls and nobody seemed to care. What luxury! As they drove home behind Crist's spirited driving horse, she could not help comparing its speed and spirit with the lumbering horse car in the city. In the city, horses had to be urged with a whip to make them go, but this horse had to be held in tightly and calmed by soothing words to keep him from running too fast. It seemed that every minute of the day had either a surprise or a thrill for her.

That evening as they sat and talked, Margaret said, "I notice that you do not have window curtains, or pictures on the walls, or carpets on the floor. Is there a reason?"

"Yes," said Rosanna, "our church believes in nonconformity—'be not conformed to this world.' The church does not allow curtains or carpets or pictures. We are instructed to practice plainness in clothing, in manners, in speech, and even our carriages are different. Our preachers continually warn us against 'worldliness.' But then, we make up partly for some of the beautiful things you have by keeping our floors scrubbed, our tinware polished, and our table linen white and beautiful. We are allowed to have beautiful flowers in the house and in the yard and garden. And we dare have beautiful horses, too. How Crist admires and enjoys beautiful horses! You noticed the horse we drove for blackberries today had plenty of spirit and he was beautiful, too."

"Beautiful," said Margaret. "His sides were so glossy you could almost use them for a mirror. As for spirit, I thought every minute he would run away, but I got an awful thrill out of it. So different from those poky, old, overworked trolley horses.

"I noticed something else," Margaret went on. "Almost everybody uses a knife more than a fork when eating. At first I was slightly shocked, but I believe I know why now. Your knives are broad at the end and your forks have only two tines. For a working man to use a two-tined fork would be too tedious and slow. They can eat faster with a knife."

"Well, I never thought of that, but that does seem like a good reason," said Rosanna.

"I notice, too, how well-behaved your children are. Why, it seems to me that all they do is eat and sleep and play and grow. I don't believe I have heard one of them cry since I am here. How do you do it?"

"First of all," said Rosanna modestly, "we believe good health comes from good food, and secondly, we insist on obedience. You see, obedience is the underlying principle of the Amish religion. We are taught to obey God as set forth in the Bible, and then we are taught to obey the bishop and the ministers, whom we feel are chosen by God to teach and direct us since they are chosen by lot."

"What do you mean 'by lot'?" asked Margaret.

"That's our method of choosing a minister. Since our ministers are men who have to make their own living, receiving no pay from the church, we have in each congregation a bishop, a deacon, and three or four assisting ministers. They are generally farmers or carpenters and cannot devote all of their time to study and the preparation of sermons. We have three or four ministers so that not too much responsibility or duty falls on any one of them.

"When a minister dies or gets too old to preach, the bishop takes a vote of the church as to whether another minister should be chosen. If the congregation votes unanimously in the affirmative, the bishop sets a Sunday, generally Communion Sunday, for the election. When the proper time comes, the bishop and one minister to assist him, withdraw to an upstairs room prepared for them. The deacon stands at the stair door and another minister at the top of the stairs. The male members then go to the deacon at the stair door and name the man they believe best qualified for the ministry. When the men have finished voting, the women pass to the stair door and mention the man they feel best qualified for the ministry.

"When all have made their nominations and the votes are counted, the deacon takes as many hymnbooks from the singers' table as there were men voted for and gives these hymnbooks to the bishop, who has counted the votes. The bishop then places a small piece of paper in one of these hymnbooks. The bishop and the ministers then go downstairs and place these books in a row on the singers' table. The bishop then calls the names of all the men voted for, and each one steps up to the table and chooses one of these hymnbooks until each candidate has a book.

"The bishop then takes the book from the man nearest to him and opens it. If the slip of paper is not in that book, the man is free. Then the bishop takes the book of the next man and opens it, and continues down the line until he finds the book containing the slip of paper with the Bible verse. The man holding that book is elected by lot as the minister chosen by God.

"The responsibility of the ministry is such a serious matter that men shrink from it. There have been a few cases where the man chosen felt his inability to fill the office so overwhelmingly that he refused to serve and begged to be excused, although this is rare. Generally ministers feel themselves chosen by God, and they consecrate themselves to His service and usually do the best they can. By this method of choosing a minister we feel that we give God the greatest possible chance to choose the right man for us and for that reason obedience is easy."

"Rosanna," Margaret replied. "Your ideas and teachings about obedience and nonconformity remind me of some of the practices of the Catholic Church. You know our sisters wear a plain black garb, which carries out your teaching of nonconformity, and the priest certainly does insist on obedience to the rules of the church."

Then Rosanna said, "Margaret, tell me something about John and William. Are they doing well?"

"William is always concerned about my welfare and happiness, and he frequently speaks of you. The priest is fond of him. In fact, he thought William should study for the priesthood, but William is set on business. You see he is clerking in a large store, and there is a young man clerking with him of whom he is very fond. I think his name is Wanamaker, John Wanamaker. They are planning now to go into business together someday and have a large department store.

Brother John is a typesetter on the *Public Ledger* and I think he is getting along well. I am a little afraid sometimes that he likes his wee drappie (drinking) too well. However, William and the priest are watching him closely. I hope they can keep him on the right road."

After they had talked freely about their different churches, Rosanna asked Margaret whether she would care to go along to preaching on Sunday. Margaret thought a moment and then said, "Since it is all in German and I can't understand it, I am sure Father Calahan would not object."

When Sunday came, preaching happened again to be at Reuben Kauffman's. They were all in the carriage ready to go soon after eight o'clock, farmers' time (always at least a half hour fast). But going to church early was not out of the ordinary for Margaret since she usually attended early mass. As they drove up the road they soon found themselves in a long procession of white and yellow carriages. As they approached the barn, it seemed that carriages in groups of twos and threes were coming from all directions. As Rosanna and Margaret walked to the house, the houseyard was already dotted with groups of men moving slowly towards the house.

Inside the house they found the kitchen and the summer house and the porches filled with women and girls. They went to the summer house to remove their wraps. Everyone was curious to know who this well-dressed, stately woman with Rosanna was. Crist's sister Sarah, glancing at Margaret, whispered, "Sister." Everybody knew that Rosanna had brothers and a sister in Philadelphia; so there was no further curiosity. Anyway, it was time to go into the house and find seats.

Lydia, Reuben's wife, recognized Margaret as Rosanna's guest; so she shook hands with her and welcomed her. Then she said to Rosanna, "I have placed two chairs in the bedroom for you and your sister where you can see and hear well." Lydia knew that for anyone not accustomed to sitting on a bench without a back for three hours was a considerable task. When they were seated, Margaret noticed that all the men in the house sat with their hats on. To her this was a peculiar sight. But soon she heard a man say something in what seemed a commanding voice and with a swish every hat was off.

In a moment he began to sing; others joined till all were singing. What Margaret thought was a command was just Yost Yoder announcing the first hymn. Rosanna explained afterwards that the men never remove their hat at preaching until the first hymn is announced and then all hats are removed at once. Margaret had never heard singing like that. It was a little like the chanting of the priests but not exactly. The unison of the men's and women's voices in the Alsatian chorales moved her deeply. When a chorale swung into a minor key it almost made her weep.

Margaret noticed everything carefully—the singing, the beginning sermon, the silent prayer, standing during the reading of the Scriptures, the regular sermon and testimonies, the prayer read from the prayerbook, the benediction when everybody, even the children, bowed the knee, and the final hymn. Although she could not understand German, the solemn countenances of those men and women, the absolute silence and spirit of devotion, filled her with a sense of divine presence. She was impressed that these people, slightly stoical, came to preaching services not for entertainment but for worship. And strange as it may seem, she felt very much at home with them.

The dinner, the moon pies, and the hot bean soup, and especially the efficient promptness with which it was served, challenged her admiration. The bean soup, made in a fifty quart kettle, had a delicious flavor she had never tasted before. Rosanna explained that bean soup made in large quantities is always better.

When the Lame Yost Yoder family returned from preaching that afternoon, they discussed Rosanna's sister. Franey commented that Margaret was tall and good looking, wore a silk dress that must have cost a lot, walked straight, and talked with a clear voice. Eli had seen Margaret at a distance, too, and was interested in what Franey was saying about her. He was rather glad next day at the dinner table when his father said, "Go over to Crist's this evening, Eli, and ask him whether he needs any seed wheat."

Eli really wanted to go over and talk to Rosanna's sister, but to go without a reason might look as though he had some particular interest. He could not have anyone think that. He had never talked to a city lady before, and he was concerned about how he would look to her.

He was astonished to find how friendly and common she was. Almost before he knew it, they were talking like old friends. She told him about the city, the high buildings, the big stores, the horsecars, and the theaters. Finally Margaret said, "Eli, I have heard that there are ghosts in this valley. Did you ever see one?"

"Do you mean spooks?" said Eli.

"Yes, that's what I mean."

"Oh, yes, I have seen some myself. About a mile below Belleville there's a little ravine called Kootcher's Hollow. The road runs through it, and often when people ride through there at night, a dog without a head runs along inside the fence. Sometimes he comes through the fence and jumps right up on the horse just back of the rider. Last fall Siever Yoder and I were coming home from a cornhusking about two o'clock at night. When we came near to Kootcher's Hollow, Siever said, 'I wonder if we'll see old Shep tonight. I'm going to call him.' 'Don't you dare,' I said, but when we were riding into the Hollow, Siever called, 'Here Shep, here Shep,' and before we could count three that headless dog jumped through the fence and right up on the horse behind Siever.

"When I saw that, I rode off at full gallop. Poor Siever urged his horse with all his might, but the horse could scarcely get off the spot. When Siever finally got out of the hollow, his horse was covered with sweat and foam. Siever was frightened almost to death.

"Really?" said Margaret, her eyes wide with wonder.

"And up on the mountains I know a big rock," Eli continued. "Under that rock, right where you can see it plainly, is thousands of dollars of money in gold. But you can't get it. The minute you go near to it a thousand snakes shoot their heads out all around it and nobody has the nerve to touch it.

"And over in the Seven Mountains there is an old hotel where wheat haulers often stop overnight. A man once lived there who stole some money. After he died, lots of men saw his ghost walking around there at night and heard him say over and over again, 'Where shall I put it?' One night a teamster who was half drunk saw him, and when he heard him say over and over, 'Where shall I put it?' the teamster said, 'You fool, put it where you got it,' and nobody ever saw or heard that ghost again. That just put him to rest."

"Eli, you frighten me," Margaret protested. "Are there any ghosts around here?"

"Well, I never saw any right here, but I have heard some pretty funny noises in the barn."

While several people in the Valley admitted they had seen things they could not explain, people thought Eli had a rather vivid imagination. But for Margaret it was a great evening. She had never seen anybody before who claimed he had really seen a ghost. It was a great evening for Eli, too. He had found a person who was deeply interested in his spook stories.

The days passed all too fast for Margaret and Rosanna. Every day brought new experiences for Margaret— a trip to the top of Stone Mountain, where the whole Valley was in plain view; a trip to the big mill with the overshoot wheel; watching four spirited horses hauling a big load of oats; the cool orchard shade where it was so pleasant to read; the delicious milk and ham and eggs and the fresh fruits and vegetables; and the greatest joy of all, the beautifully quaint little niece and nephew and her adorable sister, Rosanna.

Margaret would never forget her visit with Reuben Kauffman and with Elizabeth. They both had known Margaret's parents well. Reuben spoke almost eloquently about his friendship with her father, Patrick McGonegal, while Elizabeth spoke touchingly about her great love for Bridget, Margaret's mother.

Crist went to Belleville the last evening Margaret was with them and had said to Tommy Horton, the stage driver, "Come over in the morning. Rosanna's sister is returning to Philadelphia and wants to catch the train at Reedsville."

Next morning Rosanna listened for the rumble of the stage across the bridge. When Margaret came, that rumble filled Rosanna with joy. When she heard it this morning, her heart was pained with emotion. It signaled a farewell she dreaded to face.

When Margaret had gone, the house seemed empty, and had it not been for the cheerful prattle of little Yost and Elizabeth she could hardly have endured it. Rosanna seemed to sense something more than just the sadness of parting. Some indefinable foreboding was gnawing at her heartstrings. She felt that Margaret would come to visit her again, and for a moment her heart was light. Then the sinister foreboding returned like a dismal shadow of doom and disaster slowly approaching. She could not see the sorrow, but she felt the withering blight of the oncoming shadow.

Could it be that some unseen hand was trying to point out dangers that were lurking about her children ready to destroy them? It was that indefinable intuition which sometimes brings warnings to the minds of women but which they are not yet able to interpret fully.

CHAPTER 15

The First Sorrow

AS Bishop Shem grew older, he became stricter and more conservative. He insisted that everything had to be kept just as it was a hundred or more years ago. But there were some in the church who felt there were some things that could be changed for the better without yielding to worldliness.

Since the beginning of the church, men had worn white muslin shirts for both work and dress. At work they soiled easily and it took a tremendous amount of rubbing to get them clean. Some of the women began making colored shirts, blue or brown, for their men to work in. The bishop preached strongly against this laxity and worldliness, and even went so far as threatening excommunication if the offending ones did not put the worldly, colored shirts away. Some women did not have time to make straw hats for their men. Their husbands went to the store and bought straw hats, which were both lighter and more comfortable, and this too met with disapproval.

Some of the younger men had their carriages covered with yellow oilcloth instead of white muslin because the oilcloth protected them better in rain. This, too, was breaking the old rules, and the old rules must never be broken.

Some of the girls showed considerable pride in wearing their caps (prayer head coverings) too far back on the head and showing off their beautiful, wavy hair. They also used broader cap strings with larger bows beneath their chins. Some even became so worldly that they tied their cap strings loosely, allowing the bow to rest on the chest instead of being drawn tightly under the chin where it belonged.

All these encroachments on worldliness and manifestations of pride were very objectionable to the bishop and his supporters.

In the congregation was a bright young minister, Christian K. Peachey, who rather sympathized with these offenders. He felt that simplicity of attire was the duty of all Christians, but at the same time he felt that the principle could be preserved even if some hardships were avoided. Word slowly leaked out that Crist Peachey was in favor of colored shirts, yellow oilcloth top carriages, and store-bought straw hats, and that he was not entirely averse to the girls setting their caps back a bit to show their hair and using broader cap strings to make larger bows.

At the singings the boys and girls talked about it. Some felt that they should obey the bishop. Others felt he was too strict and that Crist Peachey was nearer right. At preaching, little groups of men engaged in low-voiced conversation, and it was soon observed that these little groups were composed of men who were either for the bishop or for Crist Peachey. There never was any open disputing. Men and women and young people just quietly took sides according to their convictions or their inclinations. This went on until the bishop felt a little uneasy about Crist Peachey and his views. One Sunday the bishop preached a pretty strenuous sermon condemning those who were not faithful to the rules and the order of the church. Crist Peachey felt the rebuke keenly, but he did not feel guilty. Many of the members felt that the sermon was aimed directly at Crist and his sympathizers. This sermon stirred things up even more than before.

When communion came, the ones siding with Crist Peachey refused to commune because there was a lack of harmony in the church. Among those who did not feel like communing were Reuben Kauffman, Ben Sharp, Little Crist, and many others and their wives. Even the bishop's own son, Yost, the singer, was on the Peachey side. Finally Ben Sharp suggested that the group see Crist Peachey and propose to him that they all withdraw and start a new church.

Preacher Crist agreed that if they were dissatisfied with the strict enforcement of the old rules and order, maybe they could advance their spiritual lives better by withdrawing. He agreed to be their minister. As the new idea of separation became known, more people expressed sympathy with Crist Peachey. The new group decided to hold their services at Ben Sharp's on the Sunday the bishop's group held the regular meeting at Nicholas Yoder's. That was the beginning of the Peachey Church, and it divided many families.

Little Crist and Rosanna and Sarah and Franey and Eli went with the Peacheys while Lame Yost and Catherine stayed with Bishop Shem. Yost left his father, while Leah stayed with him. Many families that were undecided at first eventually came over to the Peachey Church. Less than ten years after the division, the Peachey congregation far outnumbered the Old School, as Bishop Shem's group came to be called. There was no change in creed or dogma between the two factions, merely a difference in the application of the Scripture, "Be not conformed to the world."

Not long after Margaret's visit, the hot August days came with burning severity. Flies were more persistent pests than ever and harder to control. Screen doors had not yet come into use. Rosanna had a device to catch flies commonly used then. It consisted of an ordinary crock with the bottom broken out, inserted into the top of a two bushel bag. A string was tied tightly around the bag near the top of the crock to hold the bag in place. Apple butter or molasses was smeared around the inside of the crock. It was then placed where flies were thick. The flies were attracted by the molasses and went into the crock to eat. When the inside of the crock became lined with flies, someone would quickly spread a cloth over the top of the crock, shake the flies down into the bag, give the bag a twist to keep them there, and then set the crock for another catch.

But despite all precautions, children were frequently stricken with cholera infantum. Already there had been several deaths; so Rosanna watched her children with the greatest of care. One day she noticed that Elizabeth cried a little and was listless and sleepy. Little Crist called the doctor immediately, but the doctor treated the case lightly and assured Rosanna that the child would soon be all right.

By the next afternoon fever began to develop accompanied by vomiting and much internal distress. Crist went for the doctor again, but he still expressed little concern, gave a few drops to allay the fever, and assured Crist that there was nothing to worry about. He said he would drop in the next day, perhaps, to see the child.

Momly came up in the evening, and when she saw her little namesake, she said to Rosanna, *"Des Kind is schlimm"* (This child is very sick). Again Crist hurried to bring the doctor, but he was out of town. His wife promised to send the doctor over just as soon as he returned. He did not come and toward morning cramps developed and finally convulsions. As they sat by the cradle watching, applying hot compresses while waiting for the doctor, little Elizabeth breathed heavily a few times and was gone.

Rosanna's grief could hardly be described. She always felt that if a doctor had been available to give proper treatment little Elizabeth would still be with her. Rosanna felt that their great sorrow came through the criminal carelessness of the doctor. To give up her little girl, so beautiful and promising, whom she had named in honor of Momly, was a grief almost too heavy to bear.

It was not long till the corn shocks dotted the fields once more. The frosty mornings opened the chestnut burrs and turned the bright green of summer into the brown and the crimson and gold of autumn.

Since the death of Elizabeth, Momly came up more frequently. She hoped she could lighten the sorrow just a bit that weighed so heavily on Rosanna's heart. She had brought her knitting today, and as they sat knitting or patching, they talked. Momly thought she noticed the weight of Rosanna's sorrow slowly lifting and that she talked with greater freedom than she had for a long time.

When evening began to fall, Momly arose to go, and as she said good-by, she added, *"Wann du mich mohl brauchst, dan komm Ich"* (When you need me, I'll come). What a comfort for Rosanna was contained in those few thoughtful words. Elizabeth might not have been able to spell "appreciation" or define "gratitude" accurately in English, but she lived these ennobling qualities every day in her heart.

As snow flurries began again to streak the mountainside and when the fall work was done, Rosanna noticed

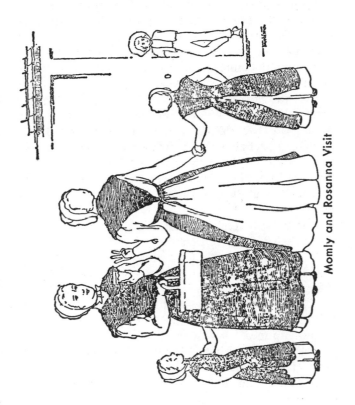

Momly and Rosanna Visit

that butter prices were improving. She decided to make all she could. During Margaret's visit and during Elizabeth's sickness, she had laid aside her undertaking to learn the twenty-four lines of multiplication. But now that her work confined her more to the house, she began again to study these advanced tables.

She was impressed with the advantage of knowing these tables. Just a week ago the butcher wanted to charge her two dollars and seven cents for sixteen pounds of beef at twelve cents per pound. But since she had already mastered the sixteenth line, she corrected him and said, "I believe sixteen pounds at twelve cents a pound would come to one dollar and ninety-two cents."

The butcher figured again and then said somewhat embarrassed, "You're right."

When she told Little Crist about it in the evening he said, "I'm glad you caught that old rascal. I always thought he'd cheat if he could. He'll think twice before he tries to cheat you again. I think I'll take you along when I go out to buy horses. Your multiplication tables might help me."

Rosanna replied with a twinkle, "These are egg, butter, and meat tables—not horse tables."

"You are right, Rosanna, they are not 'horse stables,'" Crist said, laughing. "But seriously, we must be on our guard. Honesty is part of our religion. Some people have no religion, and some who seem to have religion do not use it in business. If they can cheat a bit, they'll do it. It is so easy to be honest and to think everybody else is honest that we become an easy mark for rascals. By your knowing those tables the dealers who buy your butter and the butcher can't cheat you. If I get stuck with feed bills and horses, I'll get you to figure out my problem."

Little Crist came home from the blacksmith shop one day where he was having some new horses shod. He hurried to the house and said to Rosanna, "I have some good news for you. I have just seen the new doctor. He was at the shop getting his horse shod, and I talked with him."

"What kind of looking man is he?"

"Oh, he's a fine looking man. His name is Hudson. He is big and handsome and has a nice voice so that when you talk to him, you just can't help but like him."

"Well," said Rosanna, "you know we will need a doctor before long, and I just could not think of having that doctor that neglected Elizabeth so. If you think Doctor Hudson is all right, let's get him for when I need him."

"I hoped you'd say that. I asked Jesse Horton, the blacksmith, about him. Jesse says that he went to medical school for four years and that he is well educated. They say this other fellow went away to school only a year or two. Jesse thinks that Dr. Hudson will put the other fellow out of business and I believe it too. I'll see him soon and tell him we want him when you need him."

"My, I don't know when I was so glad. I dreaded seeing that other doctor come into my house again," said Rosanna.

Crist noticed that the news of the new doctor was a tonic for Rosanna. The burden of doubt and fear that had haunted her ever since the death of Elizabeth seemed to vanish, and she talked of the coming event with confidence and pleasure. When Crist saw Dr. Hudson one day in town, he told him that they would need him before so long.

Dr. Hudson said, "I'll be over to see your wife soon, just to get acquainted. I will give her some suggestions that may make things easier for her."

When Dr. Hudson called a day or so later, he showed such interest and concern that Rosanna's confidence in him was established at once.

When the baby was born, Dr. Hudson's skill and training soon had the child and the mother comfortable, resting, and doing well. The baby was a little boy whom they named Levi. Crist reasoned that from the sturdiness of his little body he would someday make a good harvest hand. During all these days, Momly was by Rosanna's side constantly, and she never lacked any comfort that Momly could supply.

When Rosanna was able again to look after her household duties, she found that Mary Ann Carson, her maid and friend, had done her usual splendid job of keeping the household running smoothly and everything was in order.

Little Crist went to Belleville one evening to buy the groceries, but did not return as promptly as usual. When he returned, Rosanna said, "Is anything wrong that you stayed so long?"

"Yes, I'm afraid there is. I stopped to listen to the men talking about the war, and I'm afraid some of us Amish people will either have to pay our exemption or go to war or to jail. Today Sike Brindle, Dave Fultz, Ed Stumpff, and Jesse Horton left for Washington, and they are afraid that more will be called. Lincoln called for seventy-five thousand volunteers thinking it would soon be over, but last week there was a bad battle at Bull Run, and they say the South is enlisting men by the thousands. Of course I will not go to war and kill; that's plainly against the Bible. I want to be patriotic, but between God and country, God must come first."

"But, there's another way," said Rosanna. Lincoln said that those who do not want to go to war because of conscientious scruples may be excused by paying a three hundred dollar exemption, and you know what your pap said. He said that if you are drafted and cannot pay your exemption, he will pay it for you."

"That's right," said Little Crist, "I had forgotten about that." Several Amishmen were drafted later. Some paid their exemption promptly and for those who did not have the ready cash, the church paid it.

In preaching one Sunday the bishop asked all members to remain after the singing of the last hymn and then said, "These are dangerous times. The war is raging, and we do not know who will be called next. Let us pray for deliverance from sinful requirements, but let us remain steadfast in the faith. If any one of you is drafted and you cannot pay your exemption, make it known at once to Deacon Jonas, and we will make up the money at once and free you. There is something over a thousand dollars in the alms treasury at present, and if necessary we can use that money until we have time to return it. If any man outside our church is drafted, a Lutheran or Presbyterian or Methodist whose conscience is against war and you wish to help him pay his exemption if he is not able, I believe it would be right in the sight of God. If there is nothing else, I will not detain you any longer." Then pausing a moment he added, "Go in peace."

The December winds began carrying more and more snow so that by Christmastime the mountains and the valley were covered with snow; sleighing was good everywhere. One of Crist's great delights was to hitch two fine horses to the big sled, bed it well with clean straw, cover the straw with sheepskins and blankets, bundle up Rosanna and little Yost and the baby, and go to preaching on Sunday. In most things pertaining to the Amish religion, the principle of the beautiful is discouraged rather than cultivated. When horses are well cared for, they grow beautiful, and since there never was a

Bishop Crist K. Peachey's Farmstead

church ruling against beautiful horses, Little Crist bestowed most of his aesthetical inclinations on horses. You could have a prancing team dash into the barnyard where preaching was held on a Sunday, and the team might attract ever so much attention, but since nobody could lay his finger exactly on the spot where pride could be located, it could be neither condemned nor punished.

There was some rivalry among Nancy Jake, Reuben Kauffman, Ben Sharp, and Little Crist in seeing who could drive the finest team to church, although none of these horse fanciers would ever admit that he was trying to outdo the others. Nancy Jake liked the ponderous Percherons; Ben Sharp preferred the swift-footed Hamiltonians; Little Crist leaned toward the general purpose Corn Planters, while Reuben Kauffman appreciated fine horses of any kind.

It was a pleasure now to go to preaching. The Peachey Church was growing rapidly, and there was perfect harmony between members and ministry. It was made up largely of forward-looking young and middle-aged men and women who believed in plainness and simplicity but not in too much unnecessary sacrifice and severity. Crist Peachey had been made bishop since the division, and his leadership inspired the utmost confidence in the members. He demonstrated an unusual degree of common sense, a fine conception of justice, a thorough understanding of the Scriptures, and fine tact in leadership. He was a successful farmer. He kept his one-hundred-forty-acre farm in top shape. It was well equipped with buildings, machinery, and livestock. It was all paid for, and he was known to have considerable money in the bank. His prosperity and management in material things were vital factors in establishing confidence in his religious and spiritual leadership. The Amish believe in self-sufficiency, and they strive to

The Bishop

maintain it through hard work and good management. Had he been shiftless and careless in material things, he could never have built up the strong congregation he did. But with his strong personality and his evident wisdom, his leadership was never disputed. His opinions on church affairs were eagerly accepted as authoritative and the members obeyed gladly.

Bishop Crist never resorted to anything that even bordered on coercion. Since he was called to the ministry and later to the bishopric by lot, he felt called of God, and he consecrated his life to the upbuilding of God's kingdom. No one ever doubted it for a minute. He was obviously motivated to lead out to the glory of God with no thought of personal aggrandizement, and God prospered him in every way. Neither favoritism nor revenge ever entered into the discipline of a member. Those who were disciplined felt that justice tempered with mercy was meted out to them and they were edified and satisfied. On this account his church moved forward without dissension or discord.

Life moved on pleasantly for Little Crist and Rosanna as they prospered in material things, deepened their friendships, and felt a growing sense of responsibility in the church and in the community. Experience in horse buying and selling had given Crist confidence, and with the added knowledge came both pleasure and profit. He was being recognized as an authority on horses so that younger men would ask him to go with them to appraise a horse which they were thinking of buying. They had the confidence that if there was anything wrong with a horse inside or outside, Little Crist Yoder could detect it.

Both Crist and Rosanna loved to sing, and in the long winter evenings they would often sit and sing some new chorale they had heard. Many times neighbors and friends would come just for the joy of spending an evening singing together, or to learn a new chorale that to them was especially difficult. In the preaching services Little Crist led many of the hymns. Rosanna never led any hymns in preaching services—women never did— but at weddings where women were allowed to lead hymns, she enjoyed competing with her husband. Even at weddings women were not supposed to lead any of the first three hymns, which must be sung in regular order, but after that anyone wishing to lead was free to do so.

As the years passed, more children came to the family. Three years after Levi was born, John arrived and seven years after John, Joseph, the youngest of the family, was born. Rosanna did not expect Joseph to live. He was so small at birth that he had to be carried on a pillow. Even the courageous Dr. Hudson had little hope for him. One day Rosanna said to the doctor, "Doctor, may I feed him diluted cow's milk sweetened with brown sugar?"

"Feed him anything you like," said the doctor, "He's not likely to make it anyway."

But in Rosanna's heart there was no giving up. She fed her scrawny little baby weakened cow's milk sweetened with brown sugar and, surprisingly, he began to grow. One day when Doctor Hudson came to see the baby, he said, "Why, Rosanna, this little scamp is growing. I believe you are a better doctor than I am. What did you do for him?"

"Cow's milk and brown sugar, and—you won't laugh if I tell you what else I did, will you? I asked Mattie Hartzler to come over and measure him for the 'take-off.' She found that he had it, so she powwowed for the 'take-off,' and he's been improving ever since."

"Well, I'll be hanged! I don't know what the 'take-

off' is and I don't know what powwowing is, but I know
that this little buster is getting better. And I'll not con-
demn powwowing. You Amish people seem to have a
patent on that. I heard about Dr. Bigelow when he had
erysipelas so bad that he was half afraid he'd die, and
when he finally sent for Crist King to powwow for him,
he got better at once. I believe it's a form of faith healing or mental healing, but I confess I do not understand
it. But if Mattie Hartzler can powwow for your sick little baby and help him to health, I'm for it. The time
may come when we'll all understand it better, and
maybe use it instead of so many pills and powders."

Rosanna was surprised and gratified at the sensible
attitude Dr. Hudson took toward powwowing, but no
matter what his opinion might have been or what he
might have said, nothing could shake her faith in powwowing. She herself had stopped the dangerous flow of
blood for many a man and beast when they had met
with serious accident. The neighbors far and wide knew
Rosanna's power over pain. When someone suffered
unbearably, they would come to her or send for her,
and she would powwow to stop the pain. In a few minutes the pain would be gone and the patient rested comfortably.

Bill Kosier, a hard-working carpenter, lived at the
back mountain. About every two years he would get a
very sore eye, a sort of boil on the eyeball. The Amish
name for it is *Püscht Bloder*. When the pain in his eye
became unbearable, he would come to Rosanna. After
she would powwow for him on two consecutive days,
the inflammation would clear up. The pain would disappear, and Bill would say, "Rosanna, I don't know what
in the world I'd do if it wasn't for your powwowing.
When my eye hurts so bad that I can hardly stand it, the
pain begins to ease up the minute you are through pow-

wowing the first time. You're better than any doctor. May I pay you for it?"

"Oh, no. If I took money for it, the powwowing would not do any good. If I can help you, I am satisfied." Is it possible that the faith Rosanna had in powwowing is related to the faith that can "remove mountains?" How little we really know about the possibilities of that faith described and practiced so long ago.

CHAPTER 16

The Boys

THE training of Amish children begins very early in life. The first general lesson is obedience. Parents as a rule are careful not to issue many orders, or commands, but when a command is given, it must be obeyed at once and without any back talk.

Probably the very first training in obedience and endurance comes as the child is taken along to preaching and is required to sit with his mother and keep reasonably quiet for almost three hours. The child may sleep if he wishes, but must not disturb the services. If he cries too much, he is taken out and quieted and taken into the services again. If he repeats the crying stunt too often, he is taken out of the house beyond hearing distance and punished. In that way the child is impressed that to be taken out of preaching services is no lark, and he learns to endure the long services without much complaint. To make the burden a little lighter, however, about the middle of the services the hostess comes into the room where the mothers and the children are and from a well-filled platter gives each child a piece of half-moon pie. This helps to break the monotony.

The one great virtue in Amish training is learning to work. This is done because there is always much work to do, and because of their conviction that idleness leads to wrongdoing.

At the age of six, boys are required to fill the wood-box each evening without being told to do so. It is their regular duty. At the same time they are given the responsibility of "bedding" the cow stable and tying in the cows. These tasks were assigned to Yost and Levi as they came along, and when they realized these jobs could not be neglected without reproof or punishment, they did them without complaint. To complain would be to show weakness and a lack of manly strength, and no red-blooded Amish boy wants to be a weakling. The general scorn for weaklings is a tremendous stimulus for young Amish boys and girls.

For the next few years when the March sun had dried off the fields, Little Crist took the two older boys out to the field with him to help in the first spring job—picking stones off the field that would later be mowed for hay. That job is a backbreaker, and many boys hate it, but since there were two, Yost and Levi, almost the same size, a little rivalry could be established, which helped greatly in carrying on. When the boys tired, Little Crist would say, "Come on, boys. We'll soon have this job done and then we'll begin to plow." Plowing is always a challenge for boys, and they delight in doing it, for a boy who can handle a plow and shows himself a good horseman is practically considered a young man.

As Crist saw the time approaching when the boys could work with the horses, he was careful to have on hand good reliable lead horses which the boys could work and drive without danger. One of these a roan, was called Charlie, and the other, a big bay, was named John. Yost, being the oldest, was given his choice of

Going to Preaching

leaders for plowing. He chose Charlie and that left John for Levi.

The first day's plowing was a great occasion for these boys. They did their best to see which one could plow the straightest furrow. During the first day Little Crist went first with one son and then with the other to show him how to hold the plow, how to swing it around at the end of the field, how to use words "Gee" and "Haw" to direct the horses, and how to manage the plow when it struck a rock. The boys knew all these things fairly well from following along when their father or the hired man plowed, but now to do it themselves required some practice.

When unhitching time came in the evening, Little Crist purposely remained a ways off to see whether they could unhitch and take the teams home without help. He was gratified to see these little chaps unhitch the horses properly, lead them to the fence, jump on the leader's back, and ride home. At the supper table only one subject was discussed—plowing.

"Well, I plowed more furrows than you did," Yost said to Levi.

"Maybe you did," Levi retorted, "but I plowed mine straighter than you did."

When the boys had gone to bed, Little Crist said to Rosanna, "Mother, I'm pleased with the way those two little shavers plowed today. Why, they plow as well as many grown men already. When they get a little more practice, they'll be hard to beat."

Rosanna answered with a little tease in her voice, "It's the Irish in 'em that makes 'em good workers." And as they talked of the pride and joy these two lads showed in their work, they rejoiced that their early training was already well begun.

One day as Little Crist was out in the field along the road, where the boys were plowing, Robert Maclay

drove by. As he looked in and saw these two boys plowing, he stopped and said to Little Crist, "Well, Christian
(Robert Maclay was a Scotch Irish Presbyterian gentle-
man, and he called everybody by his full and right
name), I see you are getting considerable help with
those boys plowing, and they're doing it well. You will
need more land soon. How would you like to come up
and farm one of my places? My homestead contains one
hundred and fifty acres. I'm having a little trouble farming it well, but I believe your farming would suit me
fine. Would you consider farming my homestead? Think
it over." And with that he drove away.

At the supper table that evening Little Crist told the
family what Robert Maclay had said, and as they talked
about it, the boys became very much interested in the
idea.

"Then we'd have six horses, wouldn't we?" said Yost.

Levi, twelve years old, observed, "There is not
enough work on our seventy acres to keep all us men
busy, and I'd rather farm another place than hire out to
work."

"I think Levi is right," said Rosanna, and from that
time on they seriously considered farming the Maclay
place. It was a little over a mile away, but Robert Maclay was one of the finest Christian gentlemen in the
Kishacoquillas Valley. He was Lincolnesque—tall,
slender, with a well-trimmed beard and a shaved upper
lip. He spoke slowly in low, well-modulated tones. He
was well read, lived by the Golden Rule, and possessed
a great deal of common sense. On the homestead he had
a fine white colonial house, a large barn; and apart
from one large hill, the fields were level and easily
worked.

"We will consider well before we decide," said Little
Crist, "but one thing is sure, with four boys coming on
we must have more land to farm or let the boys work

out for other people. I believe we will all be better off if we keep the boys at home." This met with Rosanna's wholehearted approval, and the decision slowly formed to accept Robert Maclay's offer.

Little Crist was amazed throughout the summer to see how rapidly the work was completed with the help of Yost and Levi, and John large enough now to do some of the chores at the barn. By the time the corn was all husked and put away and the boys were off to school, the family had fully agreed to take over the Maclay farm next year if a satisfactory agreement could be reached. Accordingly, Little Crist went to see Mr. Maclay one day to make final arrangements, if he could.

As he approached the house, Little Crist was impressed with the fine dignity of the homestead. He liked the large, white, colonial house, the towering maple trees in the yard, the luxurious garden, the well-chosen shrubbery, and the general air of culture and serenity.

As he entered the house he noticed at once the great height of the ceiling, the stately hall, the heavy rugs on the floor, the long draperies, the pictures on the wall, and the piano standing in one corner of the parlor. At first he was somewhat overwhelmed. Everything was so different from the plain Amish homes to which he was accustomed, but charming Martha Maclay, the lady of the house, soon made him forget all his timidity. It almost seemed to him that she had been expecting him and was glad he came. Indeed, Robert had told her about Little Crist Yoder and how he hoped that he would decide to farm the homestead. She called Robert from the library. He came in, shook hands with Little Crist, and made him feel like a long-looked-for guest.

Little Crist finally said, "Well, Robert, we have been thinking about your invitation to farm the homestead, and we have about decided that if you still wish us to farm it we will try it."

"Christian, this makes us happy indeed," Robert responded. "I have told Mrs. Maclay that I hoped you would decide to farm for us."

"On what terms would you expect us to farm?"

"I'll furnish the land, and half the commercial fertilizer and pay all the taxes. You furnish the machinery, half the commercial fertilizer, and do the work, and we'll divide the crops evenly. Would that seem fair to you?"

"I think that would be a just bargain and I am willing to farm for you on those terms."

"Shall I have an article of agreement drawn up for both of us to sign?" asked Robert.

"Robert, I'll take your word if you take mine and we'll not need an article of agreement."

"Your word to me is as good as your bond, and we'll not bother about the article," said Robert. "Begin work in the spring when you see fit."

For many years Little Crist farmed Robert Maclay's big farm with never a word of disagreement, and mutual respect and confidence grew deeper as the years came and went.

Farming the Maclay place not only made more work for the men, but for Rosanna, too. When they worked at Maclay's, she had to pack dinner which they took with them. But at harvesttime and threshingtime she prepared the meals at home, put the food in large kettles and crocks, loaded them into the carriage, and took them to the Maclay farm where she served them in a large, cool basement. This was hard work for Rosanna and the hired girl, but there was always a jolly social atmosphere surrounding a group of harvest or threshing hands, so the fun and pleasure of it all just about made up for the hard work.

For Rosanna there was the added pleasure of meeting Mrs. Martha Maclay, one of the most refined and cultured Christian women in all the valley. Martha Maclay graciously extended every possible favor and courtesy to Rosanna. And these two women so different in manners and customs were almost identical in ideals and aspirations. Rosanna was not quite so soft-spoken, but she cherished the same things in her heart. And Martha took such an interest in the boys that they came to look upon her as a near relative.

Rosanna's brother, John, who worked on the Philadelphia *Public Ledger,* had never been to see Rosanna. But when Margaret returned after one of her visits, she gave such a glowing account of the beautiful Kishacoquillas Valley and its quaint inhabitants, that he wanted desperately to visit his Amish sister and her family. He had heard about threshing grain, and he wondered just how it was done; so he wrote to Rosanna and told her that he would like to visit her during the threshing season.

She replied and invited him to come in September and besides seeing them thresh, he could watch them making cider, and better still, see the beautiful green of the mountains turn to still more beautiful crimson and gold.

John had never traveled much outside the city, but he recalled how some years before Margaret had told him about the close connection at Harrisburg, the change of cars at Lewistown, and the stagecoach ride to Belleville. To make the trip in one day, he left Philadelphia early in the morning. He had never seen a real mountain, and as he approached Harrisburg and saw the foothills of the Alleghenies, he was charmed with their towering grandeur. As the train roared through Jack's Narrows, he concluded that his sister must live in a mountain hut, but when he boarded the stagecoach and entered the Kishacoquillas Valley with its broad, well-kept fields, he felt he had reached the land of real "milk and honey." He saw many things he had never observed before, and wanted to ask the stage driver about them. But he decided to conceal his ignorance of the country and have Rosanna and the boys give him his information.

Crist and little Joseph met him in Belleville at the end of the stagecoach line. If Margaret had not warned him about the quaint dress of the Amish, he doubtless would have been startled when he saw Little Crist's broadbrimmed hat, his long hair and beard, and a little boy dressed just like him. But when he alighted from the stage, Little Crist approached him with a smile and said, "Are you John McGonegal?"

"Yes, sir, and no doubt you are Rosanna's husband and this is your little boy."

"Yes. Come with us," said Crist. As he led John to the yellow top carriage, John wanted to stop and look at everything. He seemed to be in a foreign land, but the gentle voice of Little Crist assured him that he was in good hands. Rosanna met John at the houseyard gate. Not until he looked into her dark eyes, observed her wavy hair, and heard the Irish ring in her voice could he believe that this was really his sister.

They had held supper until Uncle John arrived. When they were seated, he noticed that not a word was spoken, but before eating every head was bowed and a period of silence observed. Margaret had told him about the silent grace which the Amish observe before beginning a meal. He did not quite understand when Little Crist said, "Now, reach and help yourself." There was plenty in reach, but the idea of reaching for it was new. However, Rosanna came to his rescue and helped him to the most delicious ham he had ever eaten, fried eggs—dozens of them he thought—and mashed potatoes and gravy. He had never seen oven-baked bread such as Rosanna put on the table, and the butter was golden yellow.

Yost and Levi were a little shy of their city uncle. As the meal progressed, they mustered up courage to ask some questions about the city. Uncle John, for his part, was interested in their sunburned hands and faces, their long hair, and their homemade clothes. Most amazing of all to Uncle John was the air of responsibility these young Amish lads assumed toward the work of the farm. When the meal was finished and the grace observed again, the boys were off to do the evening chores. There was no conference about the work to do. Everyone knew his job, and went right at it determined to do it quickly and well.

Rosanna left Mary Ann, her trusted friend and helper, to clear away the dishes. She and her brother sat on the high front porch just outside the living room and visited. Rosanna wanted to know all about Margaret and brother William.

"Well, you know Margaret married Will Reese. I'm not so sure about him. He is a rover. Last time I heard from her, they were in Arizona with wild Indians for neighbors. But Margaret seems to be happy. She says the Indians often come with their ponies. She rides by pony to the nearby village. She says the Indians are nice to her. They call her White Swan.

"William is still in the big department store, but I am a little alarmed about his health. He is developing a cough that sounds dangerous to me. He doesn't get the outdoor exercise he should. And, now, Rosanna, tell me about the Amish. Are you happy?"

"Well," said Rosanna, laughing, "I was only five days old when I decided to turn Amish, and I really didn't have much to say about it. One of the finest women in the world took me just to help our father out, and when he never came for me, she just naturally raised me Amish. I have never known anything else.

"Don't you think I have reason to be happy? My husband is sober, religious, industrious, thrifty, and everybody thinks well of him, and I have four boys I believe will become good men. There's not much more in the world for anybody, is there?

"Of course, our clothes are not like city folks' clothes, but then when you think about it, clothes add but little and detract but little from the joys of life, as long as they are clean and decent. One thing we Amish people never worry about is changing styles. We never change the cut of our dresses. When sister was here to visit, she was fussing because her dress was a year old then and was out of style, and it made her a little unhappy. My clothes never make me unhappy. Naturally, I like to have dresses of good material, but I'm rather glad that I do not need to worry about changing styles. It must be wasteful, too, to have to throw a good dress away just because it was last year's model. We wear our dresses out, every one of them. We throw nothing away."

"But tell me, Rosanna, why don't Crist and the boys wear suspenders? I should think they'd lose their trousers."

"The church says suspenders are worldly, and for that reason they are not allowed. Besides, we make all our men's clothes, and we fit the trousers so that the waist band comes just above the hip bone. By making it a little snug, the trousers never slip down. Going without suspenders in hot weather is a little cooler and it also gives greater freedom to the shoulders in working."

"But, don't the men suffer with their long hair?" John inquired.

"Never having known any other way, they do not mind it at all. I'll admit there is no advantage in long

hair except in winter—then it keeps the ears warm—
but it is unworldly and unworldliness is the one great
principle of the Amish Church."

"I see," said John. "It is the same principle as our
Catholic sisters practice when they put on the habit.
Maybe from the religious standpoint, the Amish people
are not so far wrong, after all."

Little Crist planned his threshing to come during
John's visit. One evening he announced that the next afternoon they would bring the threshing machine and the
horsepower and set it up to be ready to begin threshing
the following morning. John was tremendously interested in seeing the big red thresher drawn by four horses
coming in the lane followed by the more modest-look-
ing horsepower. The machine was drawn to the barn
bridge, turned about, and two horses hitched to the
back of it to pull it into the barn. Then the horsepower
was placed some twenty feet from the entrance too the
barn floor. Tumbling shafts were connected to a jack
placed at the edge of the barn floor and a belt eight
inches wide connected the flywheel of the jack to the
pulley of the threshing machine.

The horsepower was a low, cog-wheeled machine
with five long, equally spaced arms extending out from
it in all directions. Two horses were hitched to the end
of each arm, so when the ten horses walked around in a
circle pulling, they furnished the power to run the
threshing machine. One man stood on the center of the
horsepower with a long whip and saw to it that each
horse pulled his share.

This threshing outfit was owned jointly by three
brothers—"Nancy Jake," "Nancy John," and Preacher
Sam Yoder—and Little Crist. They helped each other
thresh, and this cooperation was called "back help."
The mother of these three brothers was named Nancy,
so to distinguish her sons, Jake and John, from other

Jake and John Yoders, her sons were called "Nancy Jake" and "Nancy John."

Nancy John owned two farms adjoining Little Crist's farm, and he certainly did love to "feed" a threshing machine (put the sheaves into the mouth of the machine). There was quite an art in doing it properly so that all the wheat and grain would be separated from the straw.

When Nancy John and his boys arrived next morning, Little Crist introduced him to John McGonegal. After a few words of greeting, Nancy John said, "Did you bring your woman with you?"

"Do you mean my wife?" asked John.

"Yes, your wife."

Calling a man's wife his "woman" was rather unusual for John McGonegal. Afterwards he said to Crist, "I didn't know what he meant at first. If anybody in the city would ask you whether you brought your woman along you'd feel like giving him a crack on the jaw."

When the men had all gathered for the threshing, twelve in all, the driver cracked his whip, and the ten horses began to move around in the circle. John watched the tumbling shafts begin to turn. The cogwheels in the jack began to sing. Nancy John mounted the foot board. The cylinders began to whir like a swarm of angry bees. Straw began flying out of the front of the barn onto the straw stack.

Just before dinner, John went into the house and found a long table set for fourteen men (no "thirteen" business here). He wondered whether these men, so busy with work, would observe the silent grace before beginning the meal. He really was anxious to know whether their religion extended so far. In a few minutes Rosanna rang the dinner bell, and he heard the repeated "whoas" of the driver and the slowing down of the singing, shrieking wheels till everything was quiet. Then after the horses were unhitched, watered, put in the stables, and fed, the men gathered at the pump where Rosanna had placed basins, soap, and towels, and washed for dinner. When the last man was ready, Little Crist said, "Come in, men, and be seated." The men found places and waited. When all were seated, Little Crist took his place at the head of the table, bowed his head, and every man whether Amish or not did the same. John McGonegal couldn't help but respect and admire men who take their religion seriously in every phase of life. When grace was over, Little Crist said, as Amish hosts always do, "Now, men, reach and help yourselves."

John McGonegal was given a place at the end of the table where he could see everything and where he would not be jostled too much by the men. As he looked he marveled at that meal—platters filled with fried ham, stewed beef, mashed potatoes, and a rich brown gravy that would stimulate any appetite. Besides these rib-stickers there were string beans, beets, pickles, apple butter, jelly, honey, and plates of golden butter. When John thought all were filled, Rosanna brought grape pie, cherry pie, gingerbread and layer cake, but he noticed that these hungry threshers were equal to every course. He was entertained, too, by the wit and humor that passed back and forth during the meal. At threshing time one grace at the table was considered sufficient, and when the men had all finished their meal, Little Crist moved his chair back. This was a signal for all men to leave the table.

After dinner the men found a comfortable place to visit or rest or take a nap. The dinner bell rang at eleven-thirty and at one o'clock Little Crist would call out, "Time to hitch up, boys." John was surprised to see how quickly the ten horses were bridled, hitched to the horsepower, and ready to go. He noticed how the driver started the horses slowly. There was a low murmur of the revolving wheels at first, and as the speed increased, the siren song of the machine became higher and higher till it was running at full speed. This job lasted well into the second day. John wrote a short sketch on "Country Threshing" for the *Public Ledger*.

The days passed all too quickly for Uncle John, but Yost and Levi did manage to have some special treats. They took him fishing one night with the scoop net and squirrel hunting one afternoon. They went on a mountain trip to see where the chestnut trees would soon drop their bright brown fruitage. Another day they took him to the blackberry patches to see whether some late berries might still be hanging or whether they might chase a few cottontails out of the bushes. He enjoyed all these experiences immensely, but, finally, his vacation ended and he had to return to the city.

On the way home, he managed to think up a few good fish and bear stories. These he shared generously with his city pals, standing around in open-mouthed wonder, men who had never been to the country.

While Rosanna always had a hired girl to help her, nevertheless, the work necessary to run two farms was more than she could endure. One summer when she was taking harvest and threshing meals regularly to the Maclay farm, Little Crist noticed that Rosanna was more tired than usual. Mary Ann Carson's efficient work did not relieve her sufficiently; so Crist assigned young John to the house to help there two or three days each week. This helped considerably, for John had already learned to cook a fine meal and with a few suggestions from his mother he could bake fairly good bread. But even with this extra help, Rosanna caught a bad cold which speedily turned to pneumonia. Dr. Hudson, her favorite doctor, was called at once. While he was not an alarmist, he said frankly, "Rosanna, this is a serious case of pneumonia and we'll have to work together carefully." She assured him that she would carry out every suggestion, but day after day her bronchial tubes closed more and more until finally even the optimistic Dr. Hudson feared for her life. He took a special interest in Rosanna, for many times when he had cases where pain baffled him, he would send for her to powwow and relieve the pain. With her help erysipelas patients improved at once, and little children with that wasting-away sickness for which there seemed to be no medicine began eating and resting immediately after the powwowing for the take-off began. He could not afford to lose her from his community practice. He came to see her twice each day, laying on poultices, plasters, and hot and cold compresses until finally one day the tightness on her chest seemed to relax, her breath came easier, and she fell into a long restful sleep. When she awoke she said, "Doctor, I am better. That painful breathing is gone."

Dr. Hudson replied good-naturedly, "Better? I should say so. You've been getting better for the last two hours."

"What? Did I sleep two hours? And were you here all that time?"

"Was I? Well, I should say so. You were too ill for awhile for me to leave you, but now, young lady, the crisis is over, and you are better. You will soon be well again."

Those reassuring words spoken by a doctor in whom she had absolute faith, in addition to the confident look in Little Crist's face, took a load off her heart. She could feel her pulses quicken, and could almost sense her circulation carrying off the infection. After that Dr. Hudson came only once each day, and then less frequently. As he came one day, she was sitting out on the high front porch admiring the garden filled with luscious red tomatoes and the orchard red laden with apples. When the doctor found her there so much improved, he said, laughingly, "I suppose the next time I come you'll be out on one of those trees picking apples. Well, let me warn you. You've been a pretty sick young woman, and a few days' rest will be the best investment you can possibly make."

"Don't you worry, Dr. Hudson. I'm going to rest in the fresh air and sunshine till my cheeks get rosy, and Crist will make me go to work for fear I might run off and leave him."

"Yes, I can picture you running away from a husband like Little Crist and boys that show the manhood your boys do. Lady Rosanna, you're a queen on a throne, and it would take a ten-mule team to pull you off. We all know that," the doctor teased.

During Rosanna's sickness, Momly was at her bedside most of the time. She was now getting quite old and walking did not go so well. Rosanna sensed that Momly was failing rapidly, and it gave her no small concern. As soon as Rosanna had regained her own strength sufficiently she went to see Momly and was convinced that her fears had been well founded. A heart condition which she had for some years was now becoming acute at times, making her very weak.

To conserve her own strength, Rosanna had the boys hitch up "Old Charlie," the faithful old horse, to the carriage, and taking little Joseph along to open the gates, she drove down to Momly's every day. When Momly finally was confined to her bed, Rosanna asked Mary Ann Carson to come and supervise the work at home while she stayed with Momly day and night. How Rosanna loved this woman who had done so much for her, and now that Momly needed her so much, she could not leave her. Momly must have every attention of love and service that could possibly add to her comfort and happiness.

One day as Rosanna was adjusting Momly's pillow to make her more comfortable, Momly said, "My time is short now, but how glad I am that Patrick McGonegal brought me his little baby to take care of for a while. Rosanna, you have been such a good daughter to me."

Rosanna smoothed her hair and kissed her wrinkled cheek and replied, "You have done more for me than I can ever pay back. As long as I have anything, you shall never want."

Rosanna stayed faithfully at Elizabeth's bedside, but one evening as the twilight gathered in the valley, Momly's breath came slower and slower until it was no more. She did not suffer but seemed to fall into a peaceful sleep that carried her tired spirit into eternity.

When Elizabeth's body was laid away, no real daughter ever mourned her mother more sincerely than Rosanna grieved for Momly. It was the closing of a beautiful, unselfish life, and Rosanna honored and cherished her memory as long as she lived.

CHAPTER 17

Casting the Lot

AT preaching one Sunday, Bishop Crist Peachey said, "Some of our ministers are getting pretty well along in years. I would like the congregation to consider the advisability of choosing a new minister in the near future. We will take the voice of the church next Sunday, and if the vote is unanimous (all decisions must receive a unanimous vote, or the vote is lost), we will choose one on communion day, which comes in three weeks."

As Rosanna and Crist drove home from church that day, he said little, and Rosanna knew what was on his mind. He feared that the lot would fall on him and he would have to preach thereafter. Rosanna had the same strong apprehension, but wishing to ease his mind said, "How many do you suppose will be put into the lot if they make preachers on Communion Sunday?"

"Oh, I don't know, but I have an uneasy feeling that the lot will fall on me."

"I hardly think you need worry. You are already forty-four years old, and no doubt they will nominate younger men."

"Well, I hope they do, but somehow, I feel terribly uneasy." No more was said then, but on the following Sunday a vote of the church was taken on "making a preacher" and the vote was unanimous in the affirmative. "Then," said the bishop, "at the communion service in two weeks we will cast lots for preacher and may the Lord's will be done. Let us pray earnestly over this important matter that nothing may in any way hinder the will of the Lord."

When the last sound of the closing hymn died away, a great many men that day arose with solemn faces fearing that the lot might fall on them, not that they did not want to comply with the Lord's will, but because they felt the weight of the great responsibilities implied and their own sense of unworthiness.

On Communion Sunday preaching was at Dave Renno's. Knowing that communion services were always much longer than regular services, the people gathered early. By eight-thirty the house was filled and in a few minutes, Yost Yoder, the singer, announced the first hymn. Little Crist sat at the singers' table as usual, but his mind was so filled with a strange foreboding that he could hardly sing.

The preachers withdrew to the room upstairs for

counsel, as usual. The hymn ended and Reuben Kauffman began singing the *Lob Sang* (it did not need to be
announced as it is always sung as the second hymn each
Sunday) and one verse of the third hymn was led by
Ben Sharp when the ministers returned from counsel,
and the singing ended.

Old David Peachey arose to "make the beginning,"
followed by silent prayer and the reading of the Scriptures while all stood. John Peachey then spoke on the
prophets and patriarchs, which is the duty of the second
speaker. The bishop got up next and spoke of the Last
Supper, the sufferings of Christ, and the communion.

When the bread and wine had been served and the
foot washing observed, the bishop said, "According to
the vote of the church two weeks ago, it is our duty now
to cast lots that the Lord may choose a worthy brother
to break unto us the bread of eternal life. After the singing of the hymn, the members of the church may remain
seated so that we may attend to this serious matter."

After the singing of the closing hymn, all persons not
members of the church withdrew, and the ministers returned to the upstairs room where the council was held
in the morning. When all was ready, Deacon Jonas Peachey took his position at the stair door and announced,
"All the brethren who wish to place a name in the lot
will come here and give me the name." The men one
after another went to the stair door and placed a name
in nomination.

Jonas then passed the name to a minister at the head
of the stairs and that minister announced it to the bishop and an assistant, who kept account of all names sub-
mitted. When the men had all voted, the women voted
in the same manner. The bishop then counted all votes,
and any brother who had received fewer than three
votes, was dropped from the list. On this particular day
seven men received enough votes to be placed in the lot.

When this had been determined, the deacon went downstairs and took seven hymnbooks from the singers' table and carried them upstairs to the bishop, who wrote a Bible verse (Acts 1:26: "And they gave forth their lots; and the lot fell upon Matthias; and he was numbered with the eleven apostles") on a slip of paper and placed it in one of the hymnbooks. The books were taken downstairs again and placed in line on the singers' table. The bishop announced those voted for, and Little Crist Yoder was one of the seven. Each man nominated was asked to choose a book. When each man had taken a book, the bishop took the book from the man nearest to him and opened it, and if the slip of paper was not in that book, he took the book of the man next nearest, and so on till he found the book containing the paper.

When the bishop asked Little Crist for his book, Little Crist handed it to him. The bishop opened it and said, "The lot today falls on Brother Christian Z. Yoder. May God bless you and may you consecrate your whole life to His divine service." Despite his courage and his surrender to the will of God, the gravity of the office so filled him with concern that his eyes filled with tears that rolled down over his cheeks.

There was a deathlike silence and with trembling voice he said, *"Seind mir eingedenkt im Gebeth"* (Remember me in your prayers). When they were dismissed that day, many a man took his hat and went out greatly relieved. But Little Crist took his hat feeling a tremendous weight on his shoulders and an aching void in his heart.

When the men reached the yard, they gathered in groups of twos and threes and there was only one topic of conversation—that the lot today fell on one of the best qualified men in the church, obedient to all the rules of the church, and strictly "in order" (observing all regulations concerning dress).

A few of the men had the courage to come to Crist and wish him God's blessing, but Amishmen as a rule are rather reticent in such matters. All the ministers came to him, extended the right hand of fellowship, greeted him with the holy kiss, and invoked the blessing of Almighty God upon him. Bishop Peachey was especially helpful. He knew from experience what a staggering blow it was to a member to assume the duties of minister, and preach the Word of God without any particular training or preparation. But he assured Little Crist that, heavy as the burden seemed now, as he began to apply himself to the study of the Word of God, and as he understood the Scriptures more and more and became experienced in preaching the Word, the consciousness of doing the will and the work of the Lord would so lighten the load that someday it would transform these burdens into the joy of service.

Crist pondered these wise and sympathetic words during the days that followed, and they slowly lifted his burden and gave him peace.

When Crist and Rosanna returned from communion that day, it was already almost dark. The new responsibility weighed heavily on both of them. Even the younger boys noticed their mother's tear-stained eyes, and when they inquired what was wrong, she simply said, "Pap was made preacher today. He is very much broken up. Let us all be considerate of him." Even the smaller boys, John and little Joseph, only five, understood the gravity of the situation and sharing the apparent burden and gloom with father and mother, kept quiet all evening. They knew that to preach the Gospel in the German language and to be God's direct representative is a weighty and serious duty.

Fortunately for Little Crist, his boys, Yost and Levi, were now quite grown up and could easily take charge of the work both on the home farm and on the Maclay farm. John, too, was old enough to handle a team and work in the fields, so that three teams could be kept going without their father working. Consequently, day after day and night after night, Crist applied himself to the study of the Scriptures.

Bishop Peachey came down after a day or two had passed to offer further words of consolation and encouragement and direct him somewhat in his studies. An Amish minister is supposed to quote long passages of Scripture verbatim. For the next few years Little Crist literally committed whole chapters of the Bible to memory.

A newly elected minister is not required to preach at once but is given two or three months to become adjusted to his new position and duties. After awhile the bishop asks him whether he would be willing to present the opening sermon, which is only about a half hour in length. If he undertakes this short opening sermon, and finds that his preparation does not enable him to finish it, he is at liberty to sit down at any time and call upon some other minister to finish his part.

After a few attempts at "making the beginning," he is asked to preach the regular sermon, *Gemeh halde*. This sermon generally continues for an hour and a half. Again, the beginner is permitted to take his seat at any time if he feels he has exhausted his preparation, and some other minister is asked to finish the sermon. A new minister at his first attempt to preach has probably the most sympathetic audience in the world. Everybody is conscious of the tremendous difficulty of the task, and every listener is prayerfully supportive. How anxious the congregation is to find out whether he has a good voice, whether he quotes the Scriptures accurately, and whether he speaks with confidence.

The Christmas season was just beginning when the bishop said to Little Crist at preaching, "Would you be willing to try to preach the beginning sermon Sunday-a-week?"

"If you wish me to, by the grace of God, I'll do the best I can," Little Crist agreed.

The two following weeks were weighty ones for Little Crist. He redoubled his efforts. He studied more hours each day, and he studied much longer into the night. Rosanna shared the responsibility and said to the boys, "Pap has hard studying to do for the next two weeks. Let's do the work so well that he will not need to bother about it at all."

"We can easily do it," said Yost. "The field work is all done; so before school in the morning and after school in the evening we can do everything. I'll take care of the horses. Levi will attend to the steers. John will take care of the cows. Little Joseph can see to it that the chip basket and the woodbox are always well filled."

"Yost, that is a good plan," Rosanna agreed. "All that is left for Pap to do is to feed the horses at noon when you boys are at school. He will enjoy feeding the horses. Besides it will take him away from his books, give him a little exercise, and do him good. I'm a little afraid sometimes that he is studying too hard."

Each of the boys accepted his additional responsibility as a privilege just to show Pap that he meant to help him all he could. And what a satisfaction it was to Little Crist when he went to the barn at noon to feed the horses to see every horse well curried and slick as an eel, to see that Levi even curried the steers, that the cows were well bedded and clean, that the entries and "overshot" were "shoved" (cleaned with back of rake) clean, that the manure pile was built up straight on every side, and that the barnyard was raked and cleaned to perfection. Knowing how much extra work all this tidiness required, he felt a strange twitching at his heartstrings and mused, "Well, if the boys are standing by me like that, I'm going to do my best so that they will never need to be ashamed of their father's preaching."

When Crist returned to the house for the noon meal, Rosanna noticed an unusual moistness about his eyes, and she inquired, "Isn't everything all right at the barn?"

"Yes, that's just it. Everything is perfectly done. My heart is so full of thanksgiving for such loyal boys that it makes my eyes get a little watery."

"Yes, we have much to be thankful for," Rosanna agreed thoughtfully.

As the boys grow up in an Amish family, they are required by their parents to conform to the rules of the church whether they are members or not. Around the age of fourteen or fifteen, depending a little on his maturity, a boy is required to wear a *Muhtze*. When Yost, the oldest son, came to this age, Rosanna said to him, "Yost, you are about big enough now to wear a *Muhtze*. I will get you some nice black material, and you take it over to Franey Yoder and have it made. She can make good-fitting ones, and you will look smarter if it fits well."

The first Sunday Yost wore his *Muhtze* he was very self-conscious as the boys usually are when wearing their new *Muhtze*. He now looked like a full-grown man, and to avoid being too conspicuous, he sought out his friend, Joe Kanagy, who had already begun wearing his *Muhtze*. By being with Joe, he thought he would not attract so much attention.

Yost was an obedient son. He was always willing to let his hair grow long enough to satisfy the preachers, go without suspenders, wear his *Muhtze* on all occasions when he "dressed up," and at the age of seventeen, he joined the church.

But Levi, the second son, had a mind of his own.

When he had his hair cut a little too short permitting the lower half of his ear to show, and when he wore suspenders, and refused to wear a *Muhtze,* it gave his parents much concern. Many times they talked to him and urged him to conform to the rules of the church, but he could not see any good reason for doing it.

The wonderful support that Rosanna and the boys gave Little Crist filled him with confidence and courage. It gave him much the same feeling that he used to have when he hitched four fine horses to a heavy-loaded wagon and at the word to advance, every horse squared himself and crouched lower and lower so as to pull to the limit of his strength if necessary. Teamwork, ah, that's what Rosanna and the boys were showing him, and in a measure it took away his fear of preaching and filled him with confidence and strength.

As they drove to church early in the morning on the Sunday of his first attempt at preaching, he had no feeling of exultation; neither was he greatly depressed. Instead of the nervousness that he feared he might have, he felt a sort of calm composure. The gracious teamwork of Rosanna and the boys was now buoying up his hope, and his heart was filled with faith and peace.

While the first hymn was being sung, the ministers went to the council room prepared for them upstairs, and at the right time the bishop said, "Today Brother Christian Yoder will 'make the beginning,' and Brother David will preach the main sermon." As the preachers returned from council the congregation noticed that Little Crist led the procession. That meant that he would make his first trial at preaching today. Reuben Kauffman was leading that great hymn, *Weil nun die Zeit vorhanden ist* (While Now the Time Is at Hand), a hymn which Little Crist had led many times and which he knew word for word. He thought,"How appropriate. Truly, my time is at hand." The great chorale and the tremendous volume of the men's and women's voices mingling in unison lifted his apprehension and give him strength to preach the Word.

When the last sound of singing died away, he arose slowly and deliberately looked well over the audience, cleared his throat a bit and in a clear, strong voice said, "The grace of the Lord Jesus Christ be with you all. We have great reason this morning again to be filled with gratitude and praise for the wonderful mercy of God, and with the psalmist we can truthfully say, 'The Lord is my shepherd. . . .' "

He spoke clearly and with confidence and the people listened most attentively, for in that audience were scores of friends who were as anxious that he do well as he himself was. As he spoke he seemed to read their prayerful concern for him in their pleasant interested faces. He went on raising his voice a little higher and showing more and more confidence. He quoted the Scriptures well and made some appropriate comment and before he expected, the clock struck ten. He knew he had spoken the usual half hour; so he closed his remarks in the customary way, "And, so, if you are of one mind with me, let us come before the Lord in silent prayer."

Among the Amish it is not customary to comment on a sermon to the man who preached it. But after church David Byler, who was married to Franey and was Little Crist's closest brother-in-law, came to him and said, *"'Sis gute gange"* (It went well), and that was saying enough.

On the way home Rosanna also said, "It went well." Crist replied, "And I guess it went poor enough, too," but he did feel thankful that he did not need to take his seat and ask some other preacher to finish *Der Anfang* (the beginning).

CHAPTER 18

The Family

ENCOURAGED by the fact that he did not need to take his seat before the half hour was up and ask some other minister to finish the "Beginning," Little Crist applied himself vigorously every day to further Bible study as the boys went to the village school. He knew well that it would not be long now till the bishop would ask him to preach the main sermon *Gemeh halde* (literally, hold the service), and he wanted to be ready as far as humanly possible.

During the day while the three older boys were at school, the house was quiet. He accomplished much in mastering the Scriptures. Only little Joseph was at home, and he spent most of his time out of doors playing with Old Porter, the faithful Newfoundland dog, who took great pride in protecting children in general and little Joseph in particular.

When a beggar came to the gate, Old Port was right there telling him in the fiercest growl and bark not to enter. But if a neighbor stopped by Old Port would meet him at the gate with a friendly wag of his tail. If the man entered and walked toward the house, Old Port would generally pick up a stick or a bone and walk along beside him as a friendly guide until he reached the middle of the yard. Then Old Port would drop the stick or bone he was carrying. If the man stopped, all was well, but if he did not stop, Old Port would growl. If the man waited there till someone appeared to invite him in, everything was fine, but if he did not stop for the growl, Old Port would bite him and fight him off.

Once when the threshers were at Little Crist's, he warned the men not to go into the yard to pump water for the horses on account of the dog. But Sike Brindle, a husky young lad from the mountain section said, "I'm not afraid of your old dog," and in he went. Old Port met him politely, but when Brindle got half way to the pump, Old Port growled. Brindle paid no attention to him whatsoever and Old Port sprang for Brindle's throat with such a terrific bound that it almost knocked Brindle over. Brindle saved his neck by throwing up his arm, which Old Port seized by the wrist and held till Little Crist came running into the yard and called, "Let go, Port. It's all right." The dog let go, but he stood right there as much as to say, "I warned him but he would not stop. I thought it was my duty to stop him."

At first Brindle got angry and said, "I'll kill that old dog."

Little Crist replied quietly, "Would you kill a faithful watchdog for doing his duty?"

Brindle, seeing how wrong he was, walked away and said no more. He owned a few good hunting dogs himself, and when he thought a bit, he saw that the dog was entirely within his rights.

Late in the fall when summer balm was yielding to winter chill, Rosanna head Old Porter barking furiously at the yard gate. She went to see what the trouble was, and as she had expected, there stood a beggar with a large bundle on his back. Thinking he might want some food, she went to the gate to speak to him. He was a clean looking German who spoke the German language very well, and when he saw that Rosanna was Amish, he said, *"Werden Sie so gute sein mir ein wenig Mitta-gessen geben?"* (Would you be so kind as to give me a bit of dinner?)

Rosanna had been taught from girlhood never to turn

a man away hungry who asked for food; so she answered, *"Jah, des kann ich du"* (Yes, I will).

The beggar smiled at her Pennsylvania German, but he understood what she said. Opening the gate she turned to Old Porter and said, "All right, Porter," and the beggar followed Rosanna and the dog to the house. As the day was chilly the doors were closed. Rosanna did not think to let Old Porter come into the house as he often did. To guard her, he came onto the porch, stood on his hind legs, placed his front feet on the window sill, and watched through the window till the beggar was gone.

Rosanna set a good meal before this beggar—bread and butter and apple butter, ham, fried potatoes, and some other leftovers, which she had in the cupboard, and plenty of hot coffee with rich cream. So grateful was the beggar that he talked freely of the kindness and hospitality of the Amish people and when he left, Rosanna asked his name. "My name is Henry Fisher and I come from the valley of the Rhine in Germany."

After that Henry Fisher was a regular caller for years. At first he would come in the evening and ask to stay over night, and being treated courteously and never refused, he finally came and stayed over night without asking and he was treated much like any other guest. Besides supper and breakfast, he was given a clean bed to sleep in and in the evening he and the family would talk and visit like long parted friends. No man ever went away from Rosanna's door hungry.

When Rosanna was a little girl, Momly had planned that she should be a schoolteacher, but when Momly married Bishop Shem Yoder, the schoolteacher idea had to be given up. Rosanna had never quite outlived that disappointment, but as her boys went to school, she cherished a secret hope that maybe one of her boys would be apt in learning and might someday be a schoolteacher.

She soon saw that Yost, her oldest son, would never be a teacher. He took after his father in wanting to be a horseman. But Levi, the second son, liked school and got along very well. By the time he was in the third reader it was clear that he was good in mathematics. His teacher was Old Dave MacNabb, a Scotch Irishman and a devotee of arithmetic. How he delighted to watch Levi and his seatmate, John Axe, try to surpass each other in arithmetic. Many evenings John Axe would come to Rosanna's house and these two boys would work arithmetic problems till the assigned lesson was mastered. Next day when they gave perfect recitations Old Dave would say, "Boys, I'm proud of you. You're going to be men of affairs someday."

Rosanna rejoiced in Levi's application to his books. If he had an unusually difficult problem to solve, he would sit up till midnight or later rather than give it up. But she always had the feeling that Levi's ability in arithmetic was largely due to the fact that during his prenatal days she was studying the twenty-four lines of multiplication to cope with the butcher and those who came to buy her butter.

When Levi had finished the eighth grade, studying algebra and physics in addition, he took the county examination for teachers, passed, and got a school. Rosanna's cherished ambition was realized—one of her boys was a teacher!

When the school year ended and the spring work was well under way, Rosanna said at the table one day, "I believe preaching will be here in four weeks."

"Let me see," said Little Crist, "Reuben Kauffman's on Sunday, Ben Sharp's in two weeks, and then comes our turn. That makes four weeks. You're right."

To Yost and Levi, now well grown and feeling the responsibility for the looks of the place, preaching Sunday was a very important day. Many fine farmers would come to preaching, and they would notice everything about the place. These two boys intended to see to it that no one went away from Little Crist's place with cause for disparaging remarks. During the whole week before preaching Sunday they used every spare minute "redding up the place." Every board and stick had to be in its place, the barn floor cleaned out, and every piece of machinery in its proper place. The wagon shed had to be swept and every wagon and carriage lined up straight.

Then on Saturday, just preceding the service, when several women came to help Rosanna bake apple pies and half-moon pies, Little Crist gave the boys all day to finish cleaning up the premises. Every stable and entry and the "overshot" was cleaned and swept from beginning to end. The manure pile was piled up so that the sides were as smooth as a brick wall and as straight as a line in all directions, and the houseyard and the whole barnyard were swept from end to end. Every stick, stake, stone, and piece of stubble was removed so that every man as he drove into the barnyard on Sunday morning could not help but be attracted by the tidiness of the place. The preaching benches had to be taken down from their place of storage above the "overshot," dusted and washed if need be, and placed in the house to be dry and warm by morning. And the partitions between the living room, bedroom, and kitchen were removed.

When the people began to gather on Sunday morning, Yost and Levi hustled around helping them unhitch their horses and take them to the stables. They were alert for any comments, and they did not have long to wait. As they hurried the horses past men standing in small groups, they heard one say, *"Es gookt verderbt schee doh"* (It looks mighty nice here). Another, *"Doh ist es awer sauwer"* (Very clean around here), or *"Die Buwe kenne awer schaffe"* (These boys are workers). As Yost and Levi happened to pass in some unobserved place, they smiled or winked, delighted. They had their reward.

In Belleville one day Little Crist was approached by Charlie Rodgers, a witty old Irish Catholic. "Cristly, it isn't going so well wid me just now havin' considerable rheumatism and stomach misery and all," said Charley. "I'm wonderin' whether you couldn't bring me a load of fire wood someday. And would you mind speakin' to some of your Amish brethren and ask them if they would be so kind as to bring me a load, too? And if it's a frolic ye'll be havin' for me, I'll ask Molly and the girls to make ye's all a good dinner."

"I'll see some of my neighbors and maybe we can have a wood frolic for you."

"Well, if ye'll be so kind, I'm sure the saints 'll be blessin' you for your kindness."

While in town that day Little Crist happened to see Preacher Nancy John Yoder, his brother Nancy Jake, Reuben Kauffman, and Ben Sharp and they all agreed to bring Charlie a load of good cord wood or poles on the following Thursday. Later in the day Little Crist saw Charlie and said to him, "Charlie, I have seen four of my neighbors and they all agreed to bring you a load of wood next Thursday, a week from today. Will that suit you?"

"Suit me, me man? Nothing in the world could suit me better, and I'll be askin' Molly to pray the blessin' of the saints on ivery one of ye. And we'll be havin' the dinner ready for you when you get there."

On the following Thursday these five farmers went to their woodlands on the mountain and gathered up a load of wood for Charlie Rodgers. They all had about the same distance to go, and all arrived at Charlie's house about eleven o'clock in the forenoon. Nancy Jake with his fine team of dapple gray Percherons arrived first. With horses prancing, he drove into the lot with a fine load of wood.

Charlie was standing, waiting and said smiling, "Ah, begorry, Jacob, it's a fine team o' horses you're drivin' today and it's a fine load of wood you've brought me, too."

"Yes sir," said Nancy Jake. "They've about pulled my arms out trying to hold them."

The other four men arrived soon after with their own particular variety of fancy team. Knowing that Charlie had no suitable stable for the horses, they all brought horse feed, and when the wood was unloaded, fed their horses at their wagonbeds. As these five crack teams were hitched all around Charlie's modest home, old Bill Cogley, another Irishman, walked by and called out to Charlie, "By the saint's of Killarney, Charlie, are ye havin' a horse show here today?"

"Not just exactly that, but it looks enough like it. You see Molly has a birthday today and some of our Amish friends are helpin' her to celebrate by each bringin' her a load of firewood."

"Well, it's a lucky man ye aire at that for havin' a wife with such prosperous influence and friends," said old Bill.

By this time Molly and the girls had dinner all ready. She went to the door and called to her husband and said, "If the men be ready, Charlie, bid them come in."

Charlie took the head of the table and knowing that Amishmen always observe grace before beginning to eat, said, "Riverent John Yoder, would ye please be askin' the blessin'. I'm not so divlish good at it myself."

Demure as Amishmen usually are, that request just

about broke them up. Rev. John did ask the blessing
but the men all noticed that there were little hitches in
his voice which were caused by his determination to resist laughing. When the blessing was over Molly said,
"Now neighbors, ye'll be noticin' that I can't set the table
you Amishmen are used to, but the wee bite we have
you're welcome to as the flowers o' May. For the great
kindness ye have shown us today, we should be givin'
you a banquet instid o' this humble fare."

One of the men replied, "Molly, you have plenty. If
you had any more you would overfeed us and make us
sick." For years to come when these men met, one or
the other would say, "Riverent John, would you please
ask the blessin'. I'm not so divlish good at it myself."

Charlie Rodgers sounded the praises of Little Crist
and the Amish neighbors who filled his wood pile to the
limit, and it was well known that Little Crist rarely refused anything a poor man asked him for. Many a man
would come to him for a bag of wheat when poverty
was knocking at his door. Little Crist knew and the man
knew that he probably could never pay for it, but he got
the wheat just the same. More than one young woman
from the village came to Rosanna for a loan or advice,
and she never went away empty-handed.

The large scale farming which Little Crist had been
carrying on for some years—farming the Robert Maclay homestead besides his own place—was now about
to receive two serious jolts. For some years Yost had
been paying attention to Barbara Peachy, the only child
of Bishop Peachy. Barbara so charmed Yost that he
never paid any attention to anyone else, and as he became of age they were married. Their wedding was an
exact duplicate of Little Crist and Rosanna's wedding,
twenty-five years before. The marriage services were at
Dave Renno's. The wedding festivities were held at
Bishop Peachey's, the bride's home, with over two

hundred guests. There was the same menu of turkey, chicken, pie, and cake. The same three wedding chorales were sung in order after the dinner meal. Party games for the young folks were played on the carefully swept barn floor. Two boys and two girls were waiters. There were best men, the *Schnützler* (carver), the wedding presents, and finally the pseudo-collection for the cooks.

When they began housekeeping on the one-hundred-forty acre farm owned by the bishop, the homestead, Yost's gifts from home, and his dowery were exactly the same as his father had received when he and Rosanna moved into the new house Lame Yost had built for them—a horse and harness, a plow, a harrow, a cow, two pigs, a few chickens, dishes, a tablecloth, blankets, quilts, and comforters.

About this time Levi received his certificate to teach school and that left only John and little Joseph to do the work. As there was too much work on the two farms for them, Little Crist decided to give up farming the Maclay farm. He was very sorry to do this, not because of a lessened income, but because it severed his close relations with Robert Maclay. For more than ten years he had farmed this fine place and never was there a word of dissension between them. Robert was always satisfied with the work in the fields. He never questioned the division of the grain. He was pleased with the quiet, respectful conduct of the boys and men as they had occasion to work about the barn.

When Little Crist told Robert that he would no longer be able to farm his place because of two of the boys leaving home, Robert said, "I am very sorry indeed to have you discontinue. Your work and your fair dealings were most satisfactory. I shall miss your boys greatly, for I look upon them as fine young gentlemen. With Yost marrying and Levi beginning to teach, I can see how shorthanded you would be. I want to say again that to me our dealings have been ideal and eminently satisfactory."

To this Little Crist replied, "Robert, I cannot say it so well as you do, but I want you to know that I consider you a most considerate and charitable landlord. I am sorry that we are obliged to stop farming for you. Our relations have been so pleasant that both Rosanna and I will miss coming up here very much indeed. Rosanna has enjoyed so much Mrs. Maclay's kindness to her and the boys."

When Yost, being the oldest, went up to his wife's place to farm his father-in-law's farm, Rosanna missed him greatly, for up to this time the family circle had not been broken except once when Little Crist went with the bishop to Lawrence County on a preaching tour for two weeks. At that time the boys and Rosanna both missed him so much that it was difficult for them to carry on till he returned. But Yost had never been away from home, and now, for him to go off and not come home each evening was almost more than Rosanna could bear. Yost made it a practice to come home in the evening about every two weeks. Many times at the dinner table Rosanna would say, "I believe Yost will come home this evening," and sure enough, when evening came, in would walk Yost. That happened often and the family began to believe that there was some sort of connection between minds that were closely associated.

When Mary Ann Carson grew too old to make a living doing housework, the Presbyterian Church provided a home for her with someone living not too far from the church. But no matter where she was making her home, every now and then she would come to Rosanna's house and stay for a day or a week or a month. She would help a bit about the house, doing a little more than the trouble she caused. She was a light eater, and at Rosanna's house where there was always an abundance of food, Mary Ann's presence made no difference one way or the other, except she was a good conversationalist and the whole family liked her company. The boys admitted that they owed their fluent English to her.

Mary Ann was now growing quite old and the only place the church could get for her was at Lydia Esh's, and that was about two miles from church and Rosanna's house. Nevertheless, about once a month Mary Ann would walk up for a few days and then wend her way back to Lydia's house.

One day in midwinter when the snow was deep and still drifting she said to Lydia, "I hope when it comes my time to die, I can die at Rosanna's house. I have always felt so much at home there." It was only a few days after this that Rosanna was standing at the window looking out the lane marveling at the deep drifts of snow when through the snow-filled storm she thought she saw an object moving in the lane. She looked intently until the gust of wind had subsided and to her surprise she recognized the form of Old Mary Ann laboriously working her way in through the snowbanks.

"My gracious!" said Rosanna. "There comes Old Mary Ann in through the snowbanks in the lane. Somebody must go and help her at once." John seized his hat and coat and was off in a few seconds.

When he reached her he said, "Why, Mary Ann, aren't you nearly frozen?"

"Oh, no; I'm getting along pretty well."

John plowed through the snow kicking it aside to make a path for her and in a little while had her safe in the house.

When she reached the house Rosanna said, "Why, Mary Ann, weren't you afraid to start out in a storm like this?"

"No, I wasn't afraid. I somehow felt that I just had to

come today. I've been on the road nearly four hours, but I'm so glad I'm here."

That evening Mary Ann visited with abandon and contentment. She seemed to be very happy as though she had finished a task laid out for her by an unseen hand. Rosanna sensed that there was something unusual about this visit. The next day after the noon meal, Mary Ann dried the dishes for Rosanna as was her custom. When the dishes were put away she started to go into the living room, but when she reached the living room door, she fell, and when Little Crist picked her up, the muscles of her face were strangely drawn and she was unable to speak. She was paralyzed.

Crist and Rosanna quickly brought a bed down from upstairs, set it up in the living room for her and gave her the very best care and attention. The doctor said, "There is nothing to do. Make her as comfortable as you can. She cannot live more than a few days." She lived just one week. During that time a number of her church friends came to see her. She tried to speak but only Rosanna could understand what she said.

At the funeral Lydia Esh told Rosanna what Mary Ann had said only two weeks before about hoping she could die at Rosanna's house, and Lydia said with tears in her eyes, "The poor soul had her one great wish granted. It looks like divine leading."

After the funeral was over, Robert Maclay, an elder in the Presbyterian Church, came to Little Crist and Rosanna and said, "What does the church owe you for taking care of one of our members?"

It was Rosanna who spoke. "We would not think of taking anything for caring for Mary Ann. She has been our constant friend for many years and was like one of the family. Lydia Esh told me at the funeral that just a few days before Mary Ann came here this last time, she said to Lydia that she hoped when it came time for her to die she could die at Rosanna Yoder's house. She got her wish. She seemed so happy and satisfied, and during her sickness she tried so hard to tell me something but all I could really understand was, 'So glad.' No, Robert, it would be wrong to take anything for caring for an old, old friend."

"Well," said Robert thoughtfully, "I thank you for your great kindness. I am glad you told me about her wish to die at your house. I shall report her dying wish and your kindness to the church."

CHAPTER 19

The Tannery

ONE evening David Byler, who was married to Little Crist's sister Franey, came over to spend the evening. Probably there was no man whose friendship and comradeship Little Crist valued more highly than that of David Byler, usually called "Davy" Byler. He was a big, rugged man and often when he was not farming a place for someone else, he would work for Little Crist by the day. While he had opinions of his own, he was slow to express them, and no one ever saw him angry or heard him say an unkind word about anybody. Davy and Little Crist were about as close friends as David and Jonathan in the Bible. And each one of the boys looked upon Uncle Davy as about the finest man in the world.

In the course of the evening, Davy expressed some regret that he did not have a real job or work of his own, but had to do "day's work" for most of his living. Then he said casually, "I heard the other day that the tannery is to be sold and I was thinking that if I could arrange some way to buy it, I believe I would, but I cannot buy it without some help."

"Well, how would you like if I would go into partnership with you and we'll buy it together?" Little Crist offered. "I wouldn't like to see a stranger buy it anyway. The creek that furnishes water power for it runs right along my farm. If some careless person bought it, he might raise the water level of the dam and make a lot of trouble for me by flooding my fields."

"Nothing in the world would suit me better than for you and me to buy it in partnership," Davy responded. "I'll be glad to do the work and pay you good interest on your money."

"There is only one trouble about you two buying it in partnership," said Rosanna. "If you work there, Davy, I'll never be able to keep Crist at home. He'll be over there helping you all the time." The men both laughed and agreed that it might not be such a bad idea at that.

When the tannery came up for sale, Little Crist and Davy were there to try to buy it. Besides the tannery building, there were the bark sheds and the mill to grind bark, run by water power. The property also included two dwelling houses. When the bid reached twenty-four hundred and fifty dollars, Little Crist and Davy held off their next bid to make the competitor feel that they would not bid much more. Then just before the auctioneer said, "Sold," Davy bid twenty-five hundred. That was the last bid and the tannery belonged to Davy Byler and Little Crist Yoder, his backer. They were both delighted, not only because it was a good investment, but also because it gave them a new chance to work together in a common interest.

But Rosanna's prophecy came true. When Davy began working in the tannery, there were things that he could not do well alone; so Little Crist just naturally went over to help him. The more he helped, the more he saw the advantage of two men working there together. And the more he worked there, the better he liked it, until finally he said to Rosanna, "Davy needs me so much at the tannery, and I like the work there so well that I believe I will hire a boy to help Joseph on the farm, and if I manage it, I believe they can easily do the work."

"Do you remember my prophecy? I told you that if Davy worked at the tannery, you could not stay away," Rosanna teased.

Crist smiled and said, "Mother, I wish I could see into the future like you can."

Little Crist thoroughly enjoyed working in the tannery with Davy Byler. There was more "business" connected with it than with the farm work. Every day several men would come to the tannery to buy leather or to sell hides so that the social interaction was a pleasure. Besides, the hours were shorter and it gave him more time for Scripture study. Since Amish ministers receive no remuneration from the church in any way, and since Little Crist felt that he had not yet reached the stage of independence, he did feel that he should do something that would bring in a reasonable income.

When he thought back over his horse-dealing career, he was astonished to see how easy it was for him to give it all up without a struggle when once the obligations and the responsibilities of the ministry were made clear to him. Once he was so interested in the horse business that he thought he could never give it up. He still liked nice horses, but he had no desire to buy and sell and trade. His great desire now was to lay something by each year from the farm and tannery so that when the time came that he was not able to work, he would have enough on which to live and not be a burden to the state. But especially now he wanted to serve the church and inspire men and women and boys and girls to live the religious life daily.

Levi was now teaching his third term of school, and besides being good in arithmetic, he was quite an athlete. He played baseball well, but he excelled in skating. Like his father, he was good at wrestling. Skating in Jakey Hartzler's meadow attracted many boys from school, and when it came to a real race for speed, Levi could pass the best of them.

One day while he was teaching the Maclay school, Jim McCormick was having a public sale near by. It was a beautiful day in early spring. Jim's place was situated at the foot of Stone Mountain. Many people were there from Stone Valley. Because of outdoor work in the woods, the Stone Valley people were rather rugged. A husky young wrestler from Stone Valley came to Jim McCormick's sale and was downing everyone whom he wrestled. When Levi's schoolboys saw that, they ran to the schoolhouse not far away and said, "Teacher, there's a fellow from Stone Valley up here at the sale and he's throwing everybody who wrestles with him. Come up and wrestle him. You can throw him. We know you can."

"Oh, I don't want to wrestle him," said Levi. But the boys insisted. Levi had thought of going to the sale anyway (all his pupils were there), so he walked up to look this champion over. Levi soon saw that the Stone Valley champion was well built for wrestling, short, heavy and strong as a horse.

When Levi appeared, several men called to him, "We've been waiting for you. We want you to wrestle this young fellow."

"Oh, I don't care to wrestle," said Levi, but the Stone Valley champion was so eager for a match that Levi either had to wrestle or appear cowardly. Finally Levi agreed to a contest and the heavy champion smiled with a sneer that filled Levi with determination. They wrestled "side-holts." Levi chose the underhold which made him use his left hand, but the underhold held a decided advantage in hipping an opponent. From the beginning the champion threw all his strength into the match, breathing like a thick-winded horse. Since the opponent was so eager Levi wrestled on the defensive until the champion was somewhat winded, and then, catching the champion by surprise, Levi sprang forward, gave a quick turn to the right, got the champion on his left hip, lifted him from the ground, and laid him neatly on his back. Interest was so great that it almost stopped the sale, and the crowd sent up a roaring cheer.

"I demand a rematch," shouted the champion as he jumped up.

This time Levi had to take the upperhold but he got the right hand. When they were ready the champion lifted Levi off his feet and whirled him, but when Levi came down he was still on his feet. The champion repeated this tactic three times, but Levi was still on his feet and when Levi saw the champion was getting winded again, Levi swung him backwards, tripped him with his right foot, let him go, and down he went, and the crowd gave a second uproarious cheer.

The champion jumped up enraged and said, "If I can't throw you, I can lick you."

Levi faced him calmly and said, "I believe I would not try it if I were you."

And immediately several big men stepped forward and said to the champion, "You bantered this young man to wrestle. He threw you fair, now you keep quiet and behave yourself, or we'll take care of you." And the champion saw at once that he was in the wrong crowd in which to start a fight.

One day Simeon Riehl came to the tannery, called Little Crist aside and said, "Brother Crist, I have fallen into sin! I have spoken falsely about Brother John Kanagy, and I feel that I am not worthy to belong to church. I wish you would see the bishop and have me put out of church (excommunicated). I feel that excommunication is my just punishment."

"Could you not go to Brother Kanagy and make the matter right with him?" asked Crist.

"No, I feel I have gone too far so that not even his forgiveness would make it right."

"Very well, if that is your wish, I will see Bishop Peachey and tell him how you feel and what your earnest desire is."

On the following Sunday when the ministers had gone upstairs to the council room, Little Crist made known to the bishop and the ministers what Simeon Riehl had told him and that his earnest desire was excommunication.

"Did you council him to make the matter right between himself and Brother Kanagy?" asked the bishop.

"I did," said Little Crist, "but he thinks it has gone so far that even the forgiveness of Brother Kanagy would not make him free."

When the benediction was pronounced and all were seated, just before the singing of the last hymn, the bishop said, "After the singing of the hymn the members will please remain for a few minutes."

After the hymn was sung and those who did not belong to church had gone out, the bishop said, "It becomes my solemn duty today to make known to you that one of our brethren, namely Simeon Riehl, has committed sin, has fallen from grace, and has asked to be placed in the ban (excommunicated). I therefore place him into the ban and until he repents and is taken into the church again, let no member eat with him, or drink with him or have any fellowship with him whatsoever save to bring him to repentance (see 1 Cor. 5:11)."

For the next seven weeks Simeon Riehl experienced the life of an outcast. No member of any Amish church would eat at the same table with him or drink out of the same cup or take anything from his hand. Members were allowed to give him something, but were not allowed to take anything from his hand. If he had to eat anywhere where church members were present, his food was placed on a small table in another room, and there he ate alone. Even in his home he was not allowed to eat at his own table with his wife and family. He ate at a separate table or waited till the other members of the family were through.

After almost four weeks of this separation from fellowship, Simeon Riehl decided that his sins had been atoned for and that he now would ask to be reinstated into full fellowship and church standing again. He was greatly encouraged in this belief by the bishop who called to see him, and assured him that if he felt truly sorry for his sins, and would earnestly implore God's forgiveness, God would hear his prayer and would forgive. Consequently Simeon made it known to the bishop that he believed that he had fully repented of his sins, that he had been forgiven and was now ready to be reinstated to full standing and fellowship.

For the next three preaching Sundays he was required to go upstairs to the council room with the ministers and receive instruction in repentance, forgiveness, and godly living. On the third Sunday he was thoroughly questioned by the bishop, and when the bishop and the ministers were satisfied that his repentance was sincere, he was excused, and asked to go downstairs and take a seat near the ministers' bench, and be received into the church at the close of the services.

When the last prayer was over and the benediction

was pronounced, the bishop said, "Will all the members of the church please remain seated a few minutes after the singing of the hymn?" (No church business is ever transacted in the presence of persons, old or young, who are not members of the church).

When the hymn was ended and the nonmembers, including Simeon Riehl, had withdrawn, the bishop said, "We rejoice today that one who had fallen has repented and wishes to be taken into full and active membership again. *In dem Abroth* (in the council) this morning we interviewed Brother Simeon Riehl, who has been in the ban for seven weeks. We find that he has repented thoroughly, and we believe that God has forgiven his sins, and the ministers agree that he should be reinstated into full fellowship again. We will take the consent of the church, and if any one knows a good reason why he should not be taken in now, let him give his reason." The consent of the church was taken and the vote was unanimous (every church vote must be unanimous to be valid) that Simeon Riehl be reinstated to full and active membership.

The deacon went to the door and invited Simeon back in. The bishop said, "Brother Riehl, the church has heard your request to be reinstated to full membership again, and the vote was unanimous to receive you. Come forward and be received." At this request Simeon arose and walked forward to where the bishop was standing and kneeled before him. The bishop then said, "Simeon, do you confess that you sinned and that you have done wrong in the sight of God and do you ask forgiveness for your sins?"

Simeon answered, "I do."

"Do you promise in the sight of God and in the presence of these many witnesses that you will try with the help of God to keep the commandments, obey the rules of the church, and let the Holy Scriptures be the rule and guide of your life to the best of your ability?"

And again Simeon answered, "I do."

The bishop extended the right hand of fellowship and said, "Simeon, arise." The bishop then saluted him with the holy kiss and said, "I extend to you the right hand of fellowship and thereby receive you into full and regular standing in the church. May God bless and guide you in all truth by His Holy Spirit."

Simeon took his seat and the bishop, addressing the congregation, said, "Brother Riehl has seen the error of his way, has repented, and I believe that God has forgiven him. Let us all pray for him and for ourselves that we, too, may not be overtaken in sin. From now on let no member despise him, but let us all extend to him the right hand of fellowship and hold his sins against him no more."

Then, after a moment's pause, the bishop said, "We will detain you no longer," and the congregation arose and slowly left the house. Many men who for the last seven weeks would under no consideration have sat down to the same table and eaten with Simeon Riehl now shook hands with him and said, "Glad you have taken the step which sets you right with God and the church." In things religious Amishmen speak but few words; so some of the men merely shook hands, which meant, "I approve and you have my best wishes."

That Sunday evening Simeon Riehl, for the first time in seven weeks sat down to eat with his wife and family at the table. When the simple meal was ended, Simeon's little daughter, Mary, came around the table to where he sat at the head and said, *"Dadei, mir sin so froh des du wider mit uns escht"* (Daddy, we are so glad that you are eating with us again). In response to her greeting he put his strong arm around her and kissed her, but his own gratitude was too deep for words when his own child welcomed him back into fellowship.

Summer had been unusually hot. Every few days great black thunderclouds filled the sky and oncoming thunder grew more and more ominous until its tremendous reverberations filled the valley from end to end. Sometimes the storm was so violent that trees were uprooted and fences leveled and crops destroyed.

During one of these terrific storms, lightning struck Mike Yoder's barn filled to the roof with hay and grain. So intense was the heat of the lightning stroke that before help of any kind could come, it burned to the ground the hay, grain, implements, and all. The only things saved from the flames were the cows in the field and the horses, which Mike and the boys hurried from the stables. It was a pitiful sight when the smoke from the smouldering embers finally subsided. There stood the crumbling foundations, skeletons of farm machinery lying in the ashes, and the bleak, unmantled barn bridge standing out like a mocking monster. Mike was a prosperous farmer, but he was not prepared for such a catastrophe.

But the day after the fire occurred, Bishop Peachy came to see just how great the damage was. When Mike told him that the cost of the barn and the machinery was nearly three thousand dollars, he said, *"Jah well"* (meaning, I think we can take care of you). Jonas Peachy, the deacon of the church, was generally looked to as the proper person to look after a loss like this, by seeing members and receiving their contributions. The bishop went over to see Jonas to tell him what the loss was. "We must do something now to help Mike build a new barn. I will start the donations with fifty dollars, and I will speak about it at church on Sunday."

On the following Sunday after the last hymn was

sung, the bishop said, "We are sorry that one of our members, Mike Yoder, lost his barn from a stroke of lightning. He tells me that the loss of barn and machinery is about three thousand dollars. We humbly submit to the will of God, but it is our duty to share this loss and help bear this burden. Remember that the Lord loveth a cheerful giver. Brother Jonas Peachy will visit you this week on behalf of Brother Mike, and I hope your gifts will be both cheerful and generous."

When Deacon Jonas came to the tannery next day Little Crist gave twenty-five dollars and Davy Byler gave twenty-five. There was no paper on which names and gifts were published. "Let not your left hand know what your right hand doeth" is the philosophy of the Amish when it comes to giving alms. By the time Jonas had seen all the members of the church a little more than three thousand dollars had been collected. Sol Peachy and Nancy John and a few other members who each owned three or four farms gave one hundred dollars, each indicating they would give more if needed.

When Robert Maclay, the Presbyterian elder, happened to see Jonas Peachey in town one day he said, "Jonas, I understand that you are receiving contributions toward rebuilding Mike Yoder's barn. Mike is my neighbor and friend. Would you mind if I gave something towards it?"

"We never ask anybody outside our church to help any of our members in need, and we do not patronize fire insurance companies," Jonas responded. "But if you feel prompted through good will and charity to give something, we will accept it gladly and in the same spirit of good will that you give it."

"May I ask, Jonas, just why you people do not insure your buildings in regular fire insurance companies?"

"In 2 Corinthians 6:14 the Scriptures say, 'Be ye not unequally yoked together with unbelievers,' and if we join outside organizations we do not know whether they are believers or unbelievers. To be sure that we do not violate that Scripture, we refrain from joining outside organizations of all kinds. That is why we help each other in times of accident or need. For the same reason we take care of our own poor so as not to burden the state in any way. We try to order our lives so that no Amishman ever goes to jail, unless he is put there for conscience' sake. Likewise, some of our people do not even vote at election time, carrying out the idea of being a separate people as suggested in 2 Corinthians 6:17.

"Along the same line we do not go to war, for the Bible says plainly, 'Thou shalt not kill' and the New Testament in 1 John 3:15 even goes so far as to say that if a man hate his brother he is a murderer. We pay our taxes gladly, uphold the government, and obey the laws, if the civil law does not conflict with the Bible. We try to make the Bible our rule of action and conduct in religion, in business, in our social life, and in our political life," said Jonas. "I hope I have not wearied you."

"No, not at all," said Robert. "I am very glad to know the reasons for some of your practices which differ somewhat from our Presbyterian practices. I am more anxious now than ever to contribute to the building of Michael's barn, and if you will accept it, Jonas, I should like to give twenty-five dollars."

"Thank you. I shall tell Mike that you have given and how kindly you feel toward him."

Rosanna had a quilting party one day when her sisters-in-law, Sarah and Franey, and Barbara Sharp, Lydia Kauffman, and Mary Riehl came to help. They quilted in the forenoon, and at dinnertime Rosanna had a fine meal for them.

When dinner was over and "old Mary Riehl" helped Rosanna wash the dishes, she said, "My goodness, Rosanna, it must be nice to have plenty and set a nice table like you do. Since Lewis died I have hardly enough to eat sometimes."

"Well," said Rosanna, "there is plenty of alms money to help widows. Why don't you speak to the bishop about it?"

"Oh, I'm ashamed to say anything to him about it."

"All right," said Rosanna, "I'll tell Crist and he will gladly speak to the bishop for you."

When the bishop was informed about Widow Riehl's need, he brought it before the church in the regular way. The church gave unanimous consent to help her and it was not long until Jonas Peachey, the deacon, whose duty it was to look after the poor, came with money and provisions. "Mary, I want you to be saving, and make this go as far as you can, and help yourself as much as you can, but when you need wood or coal or food or money, just you let me know. You know we take care of our people who cannot provide for themselves. We never let our members go to the poor house. We take care of them, so don't worry, Mary, we'll take care of you."

Mary thanked him and said, "I am so ashamed that I have to take help, but Lewis was sick a long time before he died, and it took just about all we had for doctor bills. I am ashamed to let people know that I am so poor, but one day I was up at Rosanna Yoder's at a quilting and she had such a good dinner that I just couldn't help mentioning it to her, and I guess she told Little Crist right away and he told the bishop. I am so thankful that I will never need to go to the poor house. I thank the good Lord every day."

When Mary saw Rosanna again, she inquired, "Did you tell Little Crist about how poor I am, and did he tell the bishop?"

"Yes, I told Little Crist and he told the bishop and

that is the reason it was brought before the church. Have they done anything for you?"

"Oh my, yes. Jonas Peachey, the deacon, came the very next day after it was voted on in church and brought me a ham, a bushel of potatoes, a bag of flour, some apples, and ten dollars, and he said, 'Make this go as far as you can, but when you need more we will get it for you. We will never let you or any member go to the poor house. We will take care of you.' I'll make this go as far as I can. I don't want to be a burden to the church, but just now I couldn't help it. I pray every day that the Lord will show me a way to make my own living, for I do not want to live off the church."

"Don't worry, Mary," said Rosanna, "there is plenty of alms money. Why, I don't believe anybody needed help in the last ten years. We might just as well use the money, and, Mary, I would just as soon see you get some of that money as anybody I know of. Of course, make it go as far as you can. We all do that all the time, but don't worry about it."

Joseph was now about fifteen years old and was quite interested in school. Physiology had just been introduced and as he studied this subject, he took some delight in poking fun at his mother's powwowing. Educators did not believe in powwowing. Why should he? But when he said something disparaging about powwowing, Rosanna would smile and say, "Never you mind, Laddy. You'll need me someday."

It was Joseph's duty each Saturday to clean the stables. One Saturday, as he was hurrying to finish his work before dinner, he ran a dung fork into his foot. To save time, he did nothing about his wound till the work was finished and he could go into the house for dinner. He said casually, "Mother, I ran a dung fork into my foot."

"Well," said his mother, "you'd better take care of it, or it might get sore."

"Oh, I'll just wait till after dinner."

By the time he had eaten his dinner, the pain in his foot was becoming almost unbearable. He went into the living room and lay on the sofa, hoping the pain would stop, but it didn't. Finally, Rosanna came and said, "How's your foot?"

"It's hurting terribly."

Joseph knew that his mother could powwow and stop that pain in a minute if he would ask her, but he had sided with the educators who did not believe in powwowing. Now he was ashamed to ask her to powwow for his foot. Finally the pain became so severe that he could scarcely endure it. When the pain had overcome his pride, he said, "Mother, could you powwow for this pain in my foot and take it away?"

"Yes, I can, if you want me to."

"Well, I wish you would."

Rosanna stroked her hand across the wound three times, repeated the prescribed words that allay pain and in about two minutes the pain was gone and Joseph fell asleep. He never pooh-poohed powwowing again.

CHAPTER 20

The New House

BY this time all the boys were married but Joseph. Being a great admirer of Levi, Joseph too decided to be a teacher. When he was twenty years old, he took the county examination, passed, and was assigned a school. Since Little Crist was now working at the tannery all of the time, no one would be left on the farm to do the work. When this situation became apparent, Little Crist said, "Mother, what would you think of the idea of building a new house at the tannery, move into it, and rent our place to some good farmer?"

"Well, work doesn't go so well with me any more. I would be very much in favor of it. With Joseph beginning to teach school, we would have nothing but trouble here on the farm if we had to depend on hired help." Davy Byler was agreed to this, too. The dampness in the tannery was giving him trouble with rheumatism. Crist bought him out, so that Davy was free to do what he wished.

After planning the new house, the old house at the tannery was-torn down and the new one begun. To avoid needing to care for stock in the winter-time, Little Crist held a sale of his farming implements and livestock in the fall of the year. By pushing the work on the new house, they were able to move into it in December.

The new house was a joy to Rosanna. While there was still much work to be done—grading the yard, locating the garden, adding another coat of paint to the house, and planting flowers and shubbery, yet it was much more convenient. Little Crist now ate at home at noon instead of carrying his lunch as before. The house was as modern as an Amish house dared be, but Rosanna was sorry she could not have a bathroom, hot water heat, a telephone, and electric lights. These things were forbidden by the church as "worldly devices" and were not tolerated. However, the new house was on the edge of the village, and its nearness to the stores and the post office made living seem much more pleasant and desirable.

The new house was not built with removable partitions to accommodate preaching. They arranged with a farmer belonging to the Peachy Church to accommodate preaching services when it was their turn. Rosanna felt that she had done enough of that work during all her life, and now someone else might do the work of "taking preaching."

Joseph's school was only two miles away from home. He boarded with "Pap and Mother" helping in the evenings to get the new home in order. His first winter of teaching went well, but he soon saw that to have any hope for the best positions, he would have to have more education. At the end of the first winter he went off to college to take a teacher's course. When he went away to school, many good Amish people were truly sorry.

Deacon Jonas Peachey, who felt that he was a special friend of the family, came to see Joseph and tried to persuade him not to go. He said, "Joseph, I hear you are going away to college. I am sorry to hear it. Don't you know that colleges are nothing but worldly organizations, and they will destroy your faith? In 1 Corinthians 3:19 Paul plainly says, 'The wisdom of this world is foolishness with God'; so why offend God? At present you are leading a fine Christian life, but if you go to college, I am afraid you will lose your own soul."

Joseph heard all these words of kind advice, but in his heart he felt he must go to college. When he went away to school, he felt that if he would observe three or four fundamental principles he could prove to the Amish people that he was not losing his soul. He resolved to live as fine a Christian life as possible, to retain his ability to speak the Pennsylvania German language fluently, and to maintain his physical strength and his ability to do manual labor of the heaviest kind rapidly and well.

At the college he took part in all Christian activities. To prove his German-speaking ability he wrote a poem in Pennsylvania German, *Noch Denke* ("Reminiscing"), and had it published in the home paper. During vacations he spoke Pennsylvania German to all the Amish people he met. In order to keep physically fit in college, he took an active part in athletics. When he came home for the summer vacation, he would manage on his father's farm to take the team in the hayfield and set the pace. (Little Crist had rented the farm, but he had agreed to make hay with the aid of Sam Kinkle's big six-horse team.)

Joseph had learned that white clothing reflects the heat of the sun, so he wore a white shirt, white duck trousers, and tennis shoes while pitching hay. This gave him sure footing and kept him cooler. He always put a good-sized Amishman on the other side of the wagon to pitch hay against him, and then he would work so fast that by evening the husky Amishman pitching against him would be exhausted. The idea was to make the Amishman say, "I don't see how that Joseph Yoder can pitch hay like he does. Why he goes to college, and when he comes home, it takes a mighty good man to keep up with him in the hayfield." And that report soon spread the length of the valley, much to his credit.

Joseph studied music and learned to write it. The German chorales as sung by the Amish people in America had never been written. He wrote three of them from hearing them sung by his father, Brother Yost, and by Reuben Kauffman. He jotted down the notes on a musical staff and then surprised these men by singing these difficult chorales back to them at once—songs that had taken these men years to learn by memory.

If any farmer had any especially heavy work to do, Joseph let it be known that he would be glad to help. One day David R. Zook said, "Joseph, do you know where I could get a good man to help load manure this week?"

"Yes, I'll help you," Joseph volunteered.

"You wouldn't help load manure, would you?"

"Sure I will. I'll try to do a good day's work, too."

"Well, I'm suprised," said David, "but I'll be awful glad if you help me."

David's son Milton, who loaded with Joseph, thought he would either show Joseph a fine pace in loading or at least he would keep up to him. The weather was hot. Joseph had the advantage in height and weight and at the end of the third day, when the manure was all hauled out into the field, Milton decided that for the good of his health he had better take a few days' vacation. For a long time after that David Zook enjoyed telling how fast Joseph Yoder and Milton loaded manure for him.

"Why," said David, "I hauled the manure into the field just outside the barnyard while they began another load, but I could never catch them. I hurried, too, but every time when I got to the barnyard with the one load off, the new load stood ready to hitch to. It was the fastest manure loading ever done for me. I think these boys tried to play each other out." And David's telling it was water on Joseph's wheel.

As these reports of efficient work went over the valley, as people commented interestedly on his German poems, and as they noticed Joseph's freedom in speaking Pennsylvania German to the Amish folks, old and young, Joseph felt that he was winning his point—holding the respect and friendship of the Amish people.

He was assured more fully of this one day when Crist Hooley of Ohio, a former valley boy, now an old man, was sitting on the Hill Store porch visiting with Preacher Nancy John Yoder. Joseph happened to walk by and being fairly well dressed attracted Crist Hooley's attention, who said to Nancy John, "Who is that young man, John?"

"Oh," said Nancy John, "that's Little Crist Yoder's son Joseph."

"Well, tell me about him. He doesn't look quite like the other young Amishmen around here."

"Well, he goes to college, but Joseph is not like other young men who go to college. It does not spoil him at all. He is just as common as ever he was, and he's one of the best workers in the valley." When Crist Hooley visited Little Crist a few days later, he mentioned to Joseph what Nancy John had said about him, and Joseph was gratified to know that his plan was working—that the Amish people looked upon him with respect and confidence.

When Joseph finished his first course in school and came home, he found his mother troubled with shortness of breath and distress about the heart. Because Dr. Hudson had moved away, Dr. Bigelow was called. The doctor did not consider the trouble serious. The family thought everything would be all right soon, and were not overly concerned about her condition.

When the new house was completed, Rosanna had a great desire to have her sister Margaret and her daughter visit her once more. She wrote asking them to come up from Philadelphia in July. Margaret, who had been married to William Reese and lived in Arizona for some years, had returned to Philadelphia again. She had a daughter, Mary, now grown to young womanhood. When they wrote to Rosanna that they would come in July, she was very happy. How different this visit would be from her other visits. (Margaret had visited Rosanna quite a number of times.) On her first visit she came from Reedsville by stage; now a railroad took its place. Then Rosanna lived on the farm amid the buzz of farm work; now she lived the quiet life of the village.

But this visit was filled with the same loving interest and concern that was evident the first time she came.

Margaret now felt that Rosanna's in-laws were her relatives, too, and the in-laws looked upon Margaret in the same way.

Margaret loved to go to see Sarah Byler, Crist's oldest sister married to Yonie (Jonathan) Byler. Sarah always had beautiful flowers in the yard, in the garden, and in the house. Her house was always immaculate, and the dinners she served were a joy to any city appetite.

She frequently went to see Franey Byler, too, Crist's second sister and married to the beloved Uncle Davy. Franey, too, was a fine housekeeper, but she was not quite so interested in flowers as Sarah, nor did she keep her house quite so immaculate. It was interesting to see how Margaret Reese, the well-dressed, sophisticated woman of the city, could sit and visit with these plain Amish women of the country with mutual interest and enjoyment.

Margaret was somewhat alarmed at Rosanna's failing health—at the attacks of shortness of breath and the distress about the heart, and they talked a good deal about the probable cause. Rosanna was aware of her condition, and when Margaret and Mary were about to return to the city, Rosanna said, "If I should die soon, will you come to my funeral?"

"No," said Margaret, "we have had a fine visit again and I would rather remember you as you are now. But you will not die soon. I'm sure this heart and breathing condition will improve when you rest a while." The last statement was made to give Rosanna courage, for Margaret was really afraid that the end was not far off.

Joseph applied for the principalship of the Milroy High School and was elected, largely because the school had become rather disorderly through improper discipline and because Joseph, among other qualifications, was admired as a champion hay-pitcher. But Joseph did not use his hay-pitching accomplishments to bring them to order.

He had been instructed by some wise professors that self-control, fairness in discipline, and firmness in decisions were the big factors in discipline. He determined to try these out to the limit. In a very short time pupils with whom former teachers had trouble came voluntarily and expressed appreciation for his methods and pledged cooperation. That seemed like victory to him.

He came home one Friday evening delighted with his success as a teacher only to be met in the barnyard by his little niece, Lena, who said, "Gramma very sick, Uncle Joseph." Those childish words struck terror to his soul. He put his horse away quickly, ran to the house, and found Rosanna very sick, indeed. The doctor had given her strong medicine and for two days she had been vomiting frequently. He ran to the corncrib, got an ear of corn, shelled it, and asked the maid to roast the corn and put it through the coffee grinder, and make a tea of it as quickly as possible. She did so. When the tea was ready, Rosanna drank it and in fifteen minutes the vomiting stopped almost entirely.

Joseph said to his father, "Let's not give mother any more of that strong medicine that upsets her stomach so," and Little Crist agreed. Joseph sat by his mother's bedside all night to see that she lacked nothing which would in any way contribute to her rest and comfort. When the doctor called next day, he was told how the strong medicine had affected her, and was asked if he would mind if a homeopath were called.

"That is your privilege," said the doctor.

The homeopath doctor examined her carefully and said, "She is in the last stages of tuberculosis and all we can do is make her as comfortable as possible during her last days. She has not long to live."

Joseph thought it could not be possible that his mother who had relieved so many people in pain and distress could not find a way to cure herself. The four sons took turns, two at a time, staying by her bedside night and day that she might not want anything, but she grew weaker and weaker until Saturday noon. While her sister-in-law, Lizzie Hostetler, was at her bedside alone for a few minutes, Rosanna said, "If I get another attack of shortness of breath like I had this forenoon, it will be the last. But don't tell the boys till I am gone."

At two o'clock that afternoon her breathing became difficult, then very irregular, and finally stopped. In the presence of her husband and her four sons her spirit left her body, and Rosanna was gone. Little Crist and the boys were prostrate with grief. They could not bring themselves to believe that Mother who had meant so much to them all their lives could possibly leave them now. But it was true, and they tried to bear up under the sorrow.

Word spread quickly that Rosanna had passed away, and in a short time men and women of the church came in and took charge of everything. Two of the women washed and dressed the body. Four others looked after the cooking and baking for the dinner the day of the funeral. Crist chose four men of the church as gravediggers and pallbearers. Levi Hartzler was asked to haul Rosanna's body to the cemetery on the day of the funeral. Other men provided preaching benches to fill the whole lower part of the house on the day of the funeral. Preacher Nancy John Yoder was asked to preach the funeral sermon while Sam Peachey was asked to "make the beginning," *der Anfang.* Still others went to see the undertaker about making the coffin and taking care of the legal matters relating to the death. It was arranged that in the evening certain persons should come and sit up all night with the body.

Because it was not considered proper to make prepa-

rations for the funeral on Sunday, it was decided that
Rosanna's funeral services should be held on Tuesday
at ten o'clock. That way all final preparations could be
made on Monday. Sunday and Monday, many persons
came to view the body. Crist and Joseph were somewhat surprised when three or four young girls from the
village came to view Rosanna and one with tear-stained
eyes said, "She was so kind to me once when I needed
help that I just had to come to see her once more."

On Monday all preparations for the funeral were
completed—the bread and pies were baked, the meat
was ready, the fruits and vegetables were prepared.
Crist Peachey (not the bishop), who lived on the farm,
brought the preaching benches and late in the evening
placed most of them so that there would not be much to
do in the morning. Another group agreed to stay up all
night with the body as others had done on Saturday and
Sunday nights. So everything was attended to and made
ready through the willing services of friends and neighbors, mostly members of Rosanna's church.

The funeral took place on October twelve. It was a
beautiful sunny day, but already autumn had touched
the green of the foliage and turned it to flaming red or
somber brown. A slight autumn haze dimmed the
mountaintops, and the lazy tinkle of a distant sheep bell
lulled the landscape into rest. The sky was cloudless,
and the haze-dimmed sunshine filled the valley with
beauty and peace. Only the lowing of cattle grazing on
the hillside or the muffled bark of a distant dog now
and then broke the solemn stillness that hung over Rosanna's house that day.

By nine o'clock all those who were helping in any
way were already present to see that nothing was over-
looked. By nine-thirty many people had gathered in the
yard and were coming into the house to find seats. A
few minutes before ten, the family, Little Crist and Jo-

seph, the three sons with their wives and children, the uncles and aunts and cousins, and some unrelated friends took their places near the coffin, which was placed in the bedroom. By that time every available seat in the house was occupied.

The men all sat with their hats on, as is the custom, till Sam Peachey, who spoke first, arose, and then all hats were removed. He spoke in a general way for about fifteen or twenty minutes and then everyone except the family kneeled in silent prayer. When they arose from their knees, all stood facing the bench on which they sat while the deacon read a suitable Scripture. When the Scripture reading was ended and all were seated, Nancy John Yoder arose to preach the funeral sermon. He had lived on an adjoining farm during Rosanna's entire married life, and while the Amish rarely indulge in eulogy, he did say some fine things about her unselfish generosity, her faithfulness in the church, and her consistent Christian life.

Only Yost had joined his mother's church. The other three boys had joined the church Amish, which was a little more liberal, and this departure was more or less held against them. Three of the boys, Levi, John, and Joseph, had some misgivings that, when Preacher John had them at a disadvantage, he might give them a thorough lacing for their disobedience in not joining the church of their parents, a common practice among the Amish. But Preacher John had been present many times during Rosanna's sickness. He had seen how her sons had taken care of her every minute.

Instead of chiding them for their disobedience in not joining the church of their parents, he came out unequivocally and said, "Some of these sons may be open to criticism for their church affiliations. But I want to say that I was here almost every day during Rosanna's last sickness, and I say with all candor that I never saw sons anywhere take care of their mother like these four young men did. They were by her bedside every minute, and I am glad to bear testimony to their faithfulness and devotion. It is a high compliment to any young man to go away to college as one of these sons has done and then come home with increased loyalty and devotion to his parents."

In order to impress the bereaved ones with the necessity of righteous living, the preacher generally gives some rather personal admonitions. He often calls attention to the vacant chair, the voice that is gone forever, the broken tie of love and friendship, and the preparation necessary to meet the departed loved one in the hereafter. This personal admonition is filled with sadness, and it is sometimes rather hard for the bereaved to bear up under it.

Fortunately, there never is any singing at an Amish funeral, and that omits one emotional factor. At the close of the main sermon, the audience kneeled in prayer while the minister read the prayer from the prayerbook (the house Amish never offer original prayers). When the prayer was over, all arose and stood for the benediction and then quietly passed out of the house.

When the people were outside, certain men removed the benches from the house, and the pallbearers placed the coffin in the kitchen between the front and back doors for final viewing. The men came in the front door and went out the back door. When they had all passed through, the women came in the back door and passed out the front door. During all this time the relatives stood on the opposite side of the coffin while one of the ministers read a hymn in German (all such exercises are in high German, not Pennsylvania German). The title of the hymn frequently used on this occasion is *Gute Nacht, Mein Liebe Kinder* (Good Night, My Beloved Children), and it is probably the saddest hymn in the German language.

When the family and the relatives had looked upon Rosanna's face for the last time, the pallbearers closed the coffin. (A paid undertaker never officiates at an Amish funeral. Men of the church do all this as a loving service.) Then the pallbearers placed the coffin on Levi Hartzler's spring wagon to which Levi had hitched his gentlest horse.

The men who had charge of the teams brought up Little Crist's carriage for him and Joseph, and Aunt Katie and Uncle Jacob. Yost's and Levi's and John's carriages followed in the order of their age. Then came Uncle Eli, Uncle Yonie, Uncle Davy, and Uncle Joe and their families, and after them intimate friends until a string of carriages a half mile long followed Rosanna to her last resting place, a loving tribute of respect and admiration. The Amish are not an emotional people, but when those many friends and recipients of her favors and talents looked upon her face for the last time that day, many eyes shed tears of profound sorrow.

When the funeral procession reached the graveyard, the pallbearers carried the coffin to the grave. When the relatives and friends had gathered around the grave, the coffin was lowered, another German hymn read, and the minister said, "Let us all pray the Lord's Prayer in silence," and all hats were removed. When the prayer was finished, the pallbearers filled the grave, shaping the dirt into a mound on top, and placing temporary head and foot stones. The people went slowly back to their carriages, while the relatives and many friends returned to the house where dinner awaited them.

When dinner was over, the house set in order again, and the people returned to their homes, Little Crist and Joseph were vividly impressed with the truth of what the preacher mentioned—the empty chair and the voice that was silent.

In a few days Joseph returned to his school duties, and Little Crist gradually resumed his work in the tannery. With the aid of a housekeeper, they maintained for many years the home which Rosanna loved so dearly but was unable to enjoy for long.

Rosanna had taken a special interest in the beautiful plants and flowers in the house and the yard. The garden rose arbors and flower beds and potted plants bore eloquent testimony to her loving attention. When these began to fade somewhat for lack of proper care, Little Crist, who had never been interested in flowers before, could not endure the thought of Rosanna's flowers dying. He began to water them and care for them as best he could. As they revived and became luxurious again, his interest in flowers grew, and he determined that Rosanna's flowers should never die.

He began pruning and fertilizing and propagating her flowers until he was as much interested in flowers as any gardener. To his credit, for many years, until Little Crist's own passing, Rosanna's original flowers bloomed to tell the beautiful story of their love and devotion.

When Little Crist's hand became too feeble to care for Rosanna's flowers, others followed his instructions. When the final caravan, with tears for his charity and consideration, carried Little Crist away to rest beside Rosanna, the flowers seemed to join the quiet mourners and mutely beckoned, "Good-by and God bless you."

Thus closed the last chapter of the life of Rosanna of the Amish, and Little Crist, her devoted husband. But the memory of their devotion to each other and to the church and their untiring kindness to all who were in need will linger in the beautiful Kishacoquillas Valley for many years to come.

Supplement

The Amish described in this volume are a conservative people, who still hold to the belief that new things and innovations are worldly and wrong. That is why they have kept their manner of dress and mode of worship almost without change for over two and one-half centuries. Accordingly, they do not use automobiles, telephones, electric lights, centralized heating plants for the house (hot water or steam heat), bathrooms, or any of the modern conveniences.

However, in the Kishacoquillas Valley at present there are six distinct groups of Amish, who have the same Articles of Faith, but who have no church fellowship with each other whatsoever. Their practices vary somewhat. The two most liberal groups now allow some conveniences. The members of the various groups mingle rather freely at weddings and funerals and in business affairs, but in church affairs they have no dealings at all. No member of one group would think of trying to commune with any other group. He could not if he would.

The most progressive group holds its services in a church building, but the more conservative groups still hold their services in their houses or in their barns, if the house is not large enough. Only the most progressive group holds evening services.

It may be said to the credit of the Amish people that they are absolutely independent of the government. They pay their taxes and obey the law, but they see to it that none of their people go on relief or in any way become a burden to society. A fine example of this took place some years ago when officials from Washington came to Lancaster County where many Conservative Amish live. The officials asked the Amish farmers to sign government contracts promising to curtail their crop acreage. The Amish farmers said, "No, we don't sign government contracts, we obey the law. Tell us what you want us to do and we'll do it."

When the Amish agreed to obey the law but refused to sign contracts the officials were perplexed. They returned to Washington not knowing just what to do about it. In the autumn they returned to Lancaster County to see whether these Amish farmers had obeyed the law. They found the crops curtailed exactly according to requirement. Then the officers said, "We will pay you for the crops you did not raise." But the Amish farmers replied, "No, we don't take money for what we don't do." And they were immovable in refusing to take money from the government.

Among the more liberal Amish some of the young men and a few young women now go to college and then teach or go into business. But there are no college people among the most conservative groups.

The Amish are often considered clannish because they live in tightknit communities and do not associate freely with other people.

There are approximately thirty-five thousand baptized members of the Old Order Amish Church in the United States and Canada. The largest groups live in Pennsylvania, Ohio, and Indiana. They believe in nonconformity, nonresistance, nonswearing of oaths, and unworldliness in general. They are mostly farmers. They do not usually make much money but since their wants are few, they are seldom poor.

The Amish are law-abiding, quiet, and sober, and if everybody would live as they do, there would be no need of standing armies or police courts.

THE AUTHOR

Joseph W. Yoder was born to Christian Z. Yoder and Rosanna McGonegal Yoder on September 22, 1872, at Belleville, Pennsylvania. He was married to Emily A. Lane of Pittsburgh on February 18, 1932.

He attended Northwestern University and received his A.B. degree from Juniata College in 1904.

Mr. Yoder's teaching career started in 1895 near Reedsville, Pennsylvania, where he served as principal of the Milroy High School for two years. Later he taught in Indiana at the Elkhart Institute (now Goshen College).

He engaged in teacher institute work as music director in Pennsylvania, Indiana, Illinois, and Virginia. From 1906-19 he taught music and logic at Lock Haven Teachers College.

Because of Mr. Yoder's musical ability, he was frequently sought to lead evangelistic singing for the Church of the Brethren, Methodists, and Mennonites. He also taught many music classes for these denominations, as well as for the River Brethren and the Amish Mennonites.

In 1948 Mr. Yoder received a citation of honor from the Pennsylvania German Society for his books on Amish life. His works include *Amische Lieder, Rosanna's Boys, Amish Traditions,* and the present fascinating volume, *Rosanna of the Amish.* Having been born Old Order Amish himself, the author knew Amish customs intimately and was well qualified to write this account.

Mr. Yoder died on November 13, 1956. His funeral services were held at the Maple Grove Mennonite Church, of which he was a member.